Gospel Basics

FOR KIDS

Three to Six Years Old

By Brad Watson

The Gospel Basics
FOR KIDS

Copyright © 2018 by Brad Watson

With contributions by: Ben Connelly, Steve Hart, and Kevin Platt
General Editor: Jeff Vanderstelt
Illustrator: Heidi Wygle

Published by **Saturate**
227 Bellevue Way NE, #224
Bellevue, WA 98004
www.saturatetheworld.com

All Rights Reserved. No part of this publication may be reproduced, stored in a retrieval system, or transmitted in any form by any means, electronic, mechanical, photocopy, recording, or otherwise, without prior permission of the publisher, except as provided for by USA copyright law. Requests for permission should be addressed to the publisher.

Unless otherwise noted, all Scripture quotations are taken from the Holy Bible, New Living Translation, copyright ©1996, 2004, 2015 by Tyndale House Foundation. Used by permission of Tyndale House Publishers, Inc., Carol Stream, Illinois 60188. All rights reserved.

Scripture quotations marked (ESV) are taken from the ESV Bible, copyright © 2001 by Crossway, a publishing ministry of Good News Publishers. Used by permission. All rights reserved.

Scripture quotations marked (RSV) are taken from the Revised Standard Version of the Bible, copyright © 1946, 1952, and 1971 National Council of the Churches of Christ in the United States of America. Used by permission. All rights reserved worldwide.

ISBN: 978-1-7324913-0-4

Cover and book design | Nathan Parry
Editing | Nicole Geisland

Printed in South Korea

First Printing 2018

Expand the Experience

GOSPEL BASICS FOR KIDS

Visit **https://saturatetheworld.com/GB4K-extras** for coloring sheets, a curriculum kit, and more!

CURRICULUM KIT:

If you lead or are part of a team of who oversees training or discipling for children, grab the *Gospel Basics for Kids* Curriculum Kit.

Each kit contains a hard copy of the book, *Gospel Basics for Kids* videos, a PDF version of the book, PDF's of each chapter lesson with the coloring sheets, and *Gospel Basic for Kids* Sing-Alongs - everything you need for lesson planning and equipping your team.

Perfect for:
- **Children's ministry leaders**
- **Missional or small group leaders**
- **Bible camp or club leaders**
- **Parents**

LET'S SING!

Make each week's lesson sing with the *Gospel Basics for Kids* Sing-Along songs! Each original song was written with this age group in mind; simple, repetitive, and fun!

There is one song for each unit of *Gospel Basics for Kids*: Gospel, Identity, and Rhythms. Kids will learn the chorus and sing it each time they meet. Then they'll learn a new short verse each week.

La, la, la, let's go!

LET'S COLOR!

Enhance the understanding of each story with the *Gospel Basics for Kids* downloadable coloring pages!

The *Gospel Basics for Kids* coloring pages are uniquely designed to allow children to:
- creatively explore each week's story and themes
- further engage their place in God's story

Table of Contents

Introduction 11

The Gospel Story: Ephesians 2:8–10 16

Week 1: Who is God? | The Character of God 19

Week 2: Our Gospel Need | Creation and Separation 27

Week 3: Gospel Power | The Gospel is the Power of God to Save 37

Week 4: Gospel Purpose | God is Making All Things New 45

Our Gospel Identities: 2 Corinthians 5:18–21 52

Week 5: We are Disciples | Called to Learn from Jesus 55

Week 6: We are Family | The Father has Adopted Us as Children of God 63

Week 7: We are Servants | Jesus Served, and Jesus is King 71

Week 8: We are Missionaries The Holy Spirit Empowers Us as Witnesses 79

Our Gospel Life: Ephesians 4:1 86

Week 9: Listen | We Pray to Jesus and Listen to Others 89

Week 10: Story | We Tell the Story of God 97

Week 11: Bless | We Give and Help Others 103

Week 12: Celebrate | We Party 111

Week 13: Eat | We Share Meals with Others 119

Week 14: Recreate | We Play and Enjoy Creation 127

Appendix 135

I: Speaking the Gospel with Children by Mirela Watson 136

II: Teaching Our Children to Pray by Jeff Vanderstelt 139

III: Using the Bible Project Videos for Stories 141

IV: Using *The Jesus Storybook Bible* for Stories 142

Introduction

Missional communities exist to make disciples who can make disciples. *Gospel Basics for Kids* is custom-made to assist adults in making disciples of children during their intentional time with kids during worship gatherings, weekly small group meals (or missional communities), or at home. The purpose is not only to teach kids the gospel but to do so in a way that enables them to both apply it to their own lives and to teach it to others. We want to see kids living out their identities as missionaries, family, servants, and learners.

Philosophy

We believe our rhythms of life and identity as followers of Jesus apply to how we interact with children and how they interact with each other and the world around them. In other words, everything we're teaching "grown-ups" is also for kids!

When a child begins internalizing the values of the gospel at a young age, church in everyday life becomes normal. We want to equip the next generation of children to be members of a family of learners on mission. As we cast vision for gospel saturation for every man, woman, and child, we must first consider how we are calling our children to believe the gospel, and we must secondly consider how we will equip every child to go to every place with gospel intentionality.

Preparation

Each lesson has a section for the adult leaders that will help them understand the concepts for themselves and apply those truths to their hearts. We recommend setting aside thirty minutes before you teach this curriculum to read, study, and pray through the "Leader Preparation." Warning: This material can convict, encourage, and be transformative in your life, too!

Additionally, we recommend spending thirty minutes reviewing the lesson itself. Read through the curriculum and the stories beforehand. The time will be much more interactive if the teacher knows the story well enough to add inflection.

Lastly, if you are not leading each week, you should take a moment and look back on the previous weeks and read the section overviews. For example, when teaching the identity of *family*, the leader should read the overview for "Part 2: Our Gospel Identities." This will allow the leader to lead effectively within the context of the broader material.

Story and Discussion

The lessons are meant to be conversational. Questions should flow from kids and adults. Adults should lead children to answer questions as the kids discover the gospel for themselves and adults affirm their conclusions.

Because *The Gospel Basics for Kids* is conversational, it is also adaptable. Not all children in a missional community will be the same age or at the same place in their understanding of the gospel. This curriculum should be taught by adults who know the kids and in a small-group setting that can be a personal, relational, and adaptable time to explain the Good News fully to children.

TIP: For many children, having something to work on during the story will help them engage the story. You can use the coloring sheets for this.

You can find the coloring pages and other resources to use with each lesson at: **https://saturatetheworld.com/GB4K-extras**

Theme Verses

All three sections have key verses to be read at the end of each lesson. These passages capture the big-picture concept and root the lesson, discussion, and story in the Scriptures. You can consider making them memory verses, too.

Art Time and Activities

Each lesson includes an art project and coloring sheet to connect the story further. As kids work on these projects, keep the discussion going. Ask them questions about what they are doing and how it connects to the gospel, their identity, and rhythms of life to which God has called us.

For some lessons, we've included specific games and activities that integrate well with the lesson.

IMPORTANT: Final Art Show

The children will be collecting their art projects in their own "art box" that will stay in the classroom for the entire curriculum. On the last week the children will show it to their parents and bring it home. For week one, you will need to collect shoe boxes or ask parents to send small boxes for their kids to decorate and use throughout this curriculum.

Repeating *The Gospel Basics for Kids*

Everyone must return to the basics over and over again. The gospel is good news we need to hear each day.

Therefore, this curriculum is designed to be repeated. As kids and teachers walk through the stories, concepts, and activities multiple times, the gospel will become more clear, and new aspects of it can be taught.

For example, the first time children go through the lesson on the character of God, they might go away knowing what grace is and that God is full of grace. The next time, they might begin to understand God is compassionate, as well as gracious.

In fact, we've used this curriculum a couple of times a year with the kids in our missional community, and every time the kids learn new elements of the gospel.

If you do repeat the curriculum, be creative and use new crafts and activities. They will get tired of doing the same coloring sheet!

We have also included suggestions in the **Appendices** (page 135) on ways to enhance the stories with videos or by using *The Jesus Storybook Bible*, tips for speaking the gospel with children, and ideas for teaching children to pray.

Suggested Lesson Outline for Each Lesson

Here's a rough outline for each lesson. It's likely the story, craft, and prayer time will not fill all the time you have with the kids. This extra time is intentional. Free-play time is an important part of kids getting together!

- **Games, puzzles, or coloring sheets: 10-15 minutes**
  Get to know the name of each child and build some foundational relationships. It's a good idea to have just a few things out instead of letting the kids get into anything they want in this time. For example, have out just puzzles, or use the coloring sheet for this lesson and have the kids start with coloring.

- **Review**
  During this time, engage the kids in what you talked about last week. You can ask the questions in the lesson and/or recite the summary paragraph in the lesson.

- **Story and discussion: 10 minutes**
  The story and discussion act like a script and are meant to be relational. They might take only five minutes; it depends on the children.

- **Theme verse and prayer: 5 minutes**
  Read the verse. You could ask the kids to stand and stretch, read the verse again, and then pray together.

- **Art time: 10-15 minutes**
  The art time is a great opportunity to go over the lesson again or hit points that you were not able to during the "sit down time." Place their art project and coloring sheet into their art box when they finish. At the end of the fourteen weeks, they will take their box home.

  Group game/free play/singing: Remainder of time

> ## Extra Resources
> We've compiled videos, coloring sheets, and additional aids for this lesson and they're easy to use:
> **https://saturatetheworld.com/GB4K-extras**

Part 1
The Gospel Story

In part one, we will walk through the character of God, our relationship with God, the results of sin, how Jesus came to make us right with God, and how God invites us to live on-mission. We want kids to know who God is and what love is, so that when children hear, "God loves you!" they understand what it means. Because God is love and because He is forgiving and compassionate, Jesus comes and saves us. Because Jesus saves us and we are friends with God, we live on-mission.

This four-week section is summed up in Ephesians 2:8–10 when Paul writes, "God saved you by his grace when you believed. And you can't take credit for this; it is a gift from God. Salvation is not a reward for the good things we have done, so none of us can boast about it. For we are God's masterpiece. He has created us anew in Christ Jesus, so we can do the good things he planned for us long ago."

Week 1: Who is God?
The Character of God

Leader Preparation
The Whole Gospel

The apostle Paul wrote to the first-century church at Corinth that he "passed on to you what was most important and what had also been passed on to me. Christ died for our sins, just as the Scriptures said. He was buried, and he was raised from the dead on the third day, just as the Scriptures said" (1 Corinthians 15:3–4). This is the gospel; it's the culmination of the great story of redemption God has been unfolding since before time began. Each one of us is a participant somewhere in His storyline of redemption.

Paul reminded the church in Rome of the confidence we can have in Jesus and His work. In Romans 1:16–17, he writes, "For I am not ashamed of this Good News about Christ. It is the power of God at work, saving everyone who believes—the Jew first and also the Gentile. This Good News tells us how God makes us right in his sight. This is accomplished from start to finish by faith. As the Scriptures say, 'It is through faith that a righteous person has life.'"

On one hand, the gospel is "the power of God for salvation." Salvation from what? God wants to save us from the penalty of sin: salvation from what we've done, salvation from the power of sin, salvation for what we're called to do today, salvation from the presence of sin, and salvation for our future.

On the other hand, in saying "It is through faith that a righteous person has life," Paul is saying, in essence, that the good news is that God has the power to save everyone who walks by faith, believing God can save him or her. The good news is that God saves us as we trust in Him and not in ourselves. The means by which God does this—the righteousness that is revealed—is the life, death, and resurrection of Jesus applied to our lives by God's Spirit.

Followers of Jesus must see all of life—our lives and others'—through the lens of the gospel story. To do so, we must understand the whole gospel. The gospel is the power of God for salvation through faith in the person and work of Jesus Christ. It is for the purpose of glorifying God and participating in His mission of saturation, by the power of the Holy Spirit to make disciples who make disciples. In a right understanding, the gospel has past, present, and future implications. This week, we're considering who God is.

Suggested Lesson Outline

Here's a rough outline for this lesson. It's likely the story, craft, and prayer time will not fill all the time you have with the kids. This extra time is intentional. Free-play time is an important part of kids getting together!

Games, puzzles, or coloring sheets: 10-15 minutes
Get to know the name of each child and build some foundational relationships. It's a good idea to have just a few things out instead of letting the kids get into anything they want in this time. For example, have out just puzzles, or use the coloring sheet for this lesson and have the kids start with coloring.

Story and discussion: 10 minutes
The story and discussion act like a script and meant to be relational. They might take only five minutes; it depends on the children.

Theme verse and prayer: 5 minutes
Read the verse. You could ask the kids to stand and stretch, read the verse again, and then pray together.

Art time: 10-15 minutes
The art time is a great opportunity to go over the lesson again or hit points that you were not able to during the "sit down time." Place their art project and coloring sheet into their art box when they finish. At the end of the fourteen weeks, they will take their box home.

Group game/free play/singing: Remainder of time

> ### Extra Resources
> We've compiled videos, coloring sheets, and additional aids for this lesson and they're easy to use:
> **https://saturatetheworld.com/GB4K-extras**

Discussion

Opening: We want to use this time to learn, grow, and change. We want to learn who God is and who we are. We want to have a friendship or a relationship with Him.

Ask: If you had a friendship with God, what would that look like?

Explain: In a friendship, you know things about the other person like how they act and who they are. This week, we are going to talk about knowing God and what He does.

Pray: Jesus, thank you for the kids and our friends. God, please help us understand who You are and what You've done for us. We want to understand Your love and the Good News.

Explain: God created the whole world! EVERYTHING! God created you and me. Everything God does is good, right, and perfect.

Ask: What sort of things do you think God does?

Ask: What is God like?

Explain: Now we are going to look at what the Scriptures say about God. We are going to read the very words of God describing Himself. This is what He said:

Read: "Yahweh! The Lord! The God of compassion and mercy! I am slow to anger and filled with unfailing love and faithfulness. I lavish unfailing love to a thousand generations. I forgive iniquity, rebellion, and sin. But I do not excuse the guilty." - Paraphrase of Exodus 34:6–9

Ask: What is God like?

Lead them to base their answers on the passage you just read. You may want to ask them what mercy, grace, and love mean. Explain what those important characteristics are.

Ask: God says: "I lavish my unfailing love!" What does that make you think of?

You can share images like God's love is like syrup poured on pancakes so it overflows. OR, God's love is like an overflowing bowl of ice-cream with endless sprinkles! That's what lavish and unfailing means. His love is that good!

Ask: What does *faithful* mean?

Explain: Faithful means He always does what is good, right, and perfect. He always does what He says. He always takes care of people. He doesn't forget about us—any of us!

Ask: What does *forgiveness* mean, and what do you think it means that God doesn't ignore sin?

Explain: This means, God's desire and His inclination is to forgive and to make right everything wrong in the world.

During this discussion, feel free to read the passage multiple times.

Ask: If that is what God is like, what does God do?

Lead them to answer questions about giving free gifts, being patient, forgiving, etc. When they say things that are true about God, affirm them; tell them that is good and that they are right. Those things are true.

Share the Gospel:

In your own words, tell them about Jesus and what He has done, the grace and mercy we receive from God, and His forgiveness and love. If you're unsure how to do this, use Appendix One (page 128) as a guide. Or you could say something like this:

"God is so loving that He sent Jesus into the world to forgive us, care for the world, and make us whole. Jesus lived a life of love, died because of His love for us, and rose again. If we believe in Him, we live forever as people restored by God who get to tell everyone about how great God is."

Read the Theme Verse:

Ephesians 2:8–10: "God saved you by his grace when you believed. And you can't take credit for this; it is a gift from God. Salvation is not a reward for the good things we have done, so none of us can boast about it. For we are God's masterpiece. He has created us anew in Christ Jesus, so we can do the good things he planned for us long ago."

Prayer:

Ask them to share things for which they want to pray. Pray as a group; encourage them to pray, as well. See Appendix Two (page 139) for more on how to teach children to pray.

Art Project: Art Project Collection Box

Explain: For our first art project, we're going to make and decorate a box that will store all our future art projects as we learn about who God is, what He has done for us, and how we live.

In the end, it is going to be a beautiful collection of art that will help you explain the gospel to your parents, siblings, and friends.

Supplies:
- Boxes (collect shoe boxes or ask each parent to send a box with their kids for the first lesson)
- Construction paper
- Glue sticks
- Glitter/sequins
- Crayons and markers
- The template "My Art Box, by _____"

Week 2: Our Gospel Need
Creation & Separation

Leaders Preparation
Jesus Did it Better

In Romans 3:23, Paul tells us, "For everyone has sinned; we all fall short of God's glorious standard." To sin is to think, believe, or act in any way that is not like God or is not in submission to what God commands. We all have fallen short; every one of us has sinned. "The wages of sin is death" (Romans 6:23a). The result of our sin is damage to ourselves, brokenness in our relationships, destruction to the world around us, death to our physical bodies, and, ultimately, an eternal spiritual death and separation forever from a relationship with God, the giver and sustainer of life. Our rebellion, our sin, leads to brokenness.

"But the free gift of God is eternal life through Christ Jesus our Lord" (Romans 6:23b). God has made a way to give us something different than what we deserve. Since no natural human being ever has lived or ever will live a life perfectly glorifying to God, Jesus came and took on flesh as the God-man. Jesus became for humanity the true and better human, the true Son of Man and Son of God. He submitted Himself perfectly to God the Father. He obeyed Him in everything, doing only what God the Father told Him to do. This perfect obedience—this perfect life—has been given to us. Jesus is the gift of God to humanity (John 3:16). This is good news!

By faith in Jesus, you and I are saved from the need to live a perfect life to gain God's approval. Paul says that our lives are now hidden with Christ in God (Colossians 3:3). That means that if by faith you have trusted Jesus as the One who perfectly obeyed God on your behalf, God sees Jesus's performance as yours. He accepts you because of Jesus.

Do you believe—or live as if—you have to perform well for God in order to receive His loving acceptance? Do you believe God loves you more when you obey and less when you disobey? If so, how can this be understood as disbelief in what Jesus has already done?

Suggested Lesson Outline

Here's a rough outline for this lesson. It's likely the story, craft, and prayer time will not fill all the time you have with the kids. This extra time is intentional. Free-play time is an important part of kids getting together!

Games, puzzles, or coloring sheets: 10-15 minutes
Get to know the name of each child and build some foundational relationships. It's a good idea to have just a few things out instead of letting the kids get into anything they want in this time. For example, have out just puzzles, or use the coloring sheet for this lesson and have the kids start with coloring.

Review
During this time, engage the kids in what you talked about last week. You can ask the questions in the lesson and/or recite the summary paragraph in the lesson.

Story and discussion: 10 minutes
The story and discussion act like a script and are meant to be relational. They might take only five minutes; it depends on the children.

Theme verse and prayer: 5 minutes
Read the verse. You could ask the kids to stand and stretch, read the verse again, and then pray together.

Art time: 10-15 minutes
The art time is a great opportunity to go over the lesson again or hit points that you were not able to during the "sit down time." Place their art project and coloring sheet into their art box when they finish. At the end of the fourteen weeks, they will take their box home.

Group game/free play/singing: Remainder of time

> ### Extra Resources
> We've compiled videos, coloring sheets, and additional aids for this lesson and they're easy to use:
> https://saturatetheworld.com/GB4K-extras

Review

Teacher's Review: Last week's lesson was about how God created the world, and about His character. The kids heard about God being compassionate, forgiving, loving, and gracious. Last week they also heard the gospel in brief...

God is so forgiving and compassionate and loving that He sent Jesus into the world to forgive us, care for the world, and love us. Jesus lived a life of love, died because of His love for us, and rose again. If we believe in Him, we live forever as people restored by God who get to tell everyone about how great God is.

Ask: What do you remember about last week?

God is really good. He is merciful, gracious, loving, and forgiving.

Ask Follow-Up Questions:

What is *compassion*? *Mercy*? *Forgiveness*?

Remind the kids of the previous week's lesson. Don't be discouraged if they don't remember as much as you think they should. Kids are amazing and surprising. They are learning!

Diving into Our Gospel Need

Explain: God created everything. In the beginning, it was good! He made trees, the sun, and the moon. He made the animals and the creatures. He made us! We were created to love God and love others, but we are separated from God because of sin. Because of sin, we don't love others.

STORY: Creation & Separation

As you engage the story, pause, ask questions that come to you as you interact with the kids, and clarify concepts that might be confusing.

In the beginning, when God created the world, He made the first people. God said, "Let us make man in our image," and He formed the dust of the ground together and breathed into it the breath of life. God spoke to Adam and Eve and told them to enjoy all He had created: the animals, the flavors, the sights, and the work. Adam and all the humans were created with the ability to enjoy this wonderful environment God had fashioned. They were also created with the great task of reflecting the King's goodness and greatness throughout all of creation.

God made it clear to Adam there were two trees in the center of the garden. One was the Tree of Life. The fruit from this tree was to be enjoyed and eaten just like the rest of the trees. The other tree, known as the Knowledge of Good and Evil, was the only tree from which they were not to eat. If Adam ate of this tree, he would surely die.

One day a deceitful, lying serpent approached Eve and asked her a question. He asked, "Did God really say you couldn't eat of any of the fruit in this garden?" Eve told him, "No, that's not what God said. We can eat from any tree in the garden. It's only the Tree of the Knowledge of Good and Evil that we are not allowed to eat from—or even touch—or we will definitely die."

The serpent lied to Eve and said, "You won't die! God just knows that as soon as you eat from that tree, your eyes will be opened. You will become just like Him. You will be able to determine what is right and wrong for yourselves."

"Hmm. I would be able to decide what is right and wrong?" Eve thought. She looked at the delicious fruit, contemplating the decision, and she believed the lies of the serpent over the words of the good God. She reached out her hand and ate some of the fruit. Then she gave some to her husband, Adam, who was there with her, and he ate it as well. At that moment their eyes were opened, and they were flooded with guilt and shame. They quickly tied fig leaves together to cover up their nakedness. They had rebelled and chosen to live outside the good reign of God, immediately experiencing the devastating effects of that choice.

Later that day, Adam and Eve heard God walking in the garden as He always did that time of day. When they heard Him, their shame caused them to try to hide behind some of the nearby bushes.

God called out to them, "Adam, where are you?" Ashamed, Adam answered, "I heard you coming, and I was afraid because I was naked." God asked, "Who told you that you were naked? Did you eat the fruit I told you not to?" Adam replied to God, "It was the woman you gave to me—she handed me the fruit." Then God said to Eve, "How could you do this?" Eve said, "The serpent tricked me into eating the fruit."

God then spoke to the serpent. "You are cursed because you have done this. You will now be the enemy of the woman and her offspring. You will bite at his heels, but he will crush your head!"

Then God turned to Adam and Eve. He knew His good creation would be drastically affected by their choice to live outside His good reign. He knew they would be subjected to sickness, pain, suffering, and even death as a result of their decisions. Because He is just and good and cannot allow injustice or rebellion to remain in His presence forever, He had to punish them for their rebellion.

He told them the consequences of their sin:

- Women will have great pain in bearing children.
- Men will struggle, toil, and sweat while trying to cultivate the land—only to get a little bit of food from it.
- They would both struggle for power in their relationship.
- They would die and return to the dust from which they were formed.

Ask the kids to retell the story in their own words. Ask, "Who were Adam and Eve, and what happened in this story with them and God?"

Explain: In the beginning, humans walked with God and had a great relationship with each other. They had good jobs and good food—God provided everything they needed. They had names, and life had meaning.

Ask: What do you think life was like for Adam and Eve?

However, in the very middle of that life was the choice to obey and trust God or to disobey and reject God.

Ask: Do you think you have that same choice in the middle of your life today?

Explain: God warned them, saying, "If you eat of that tree, you will die." The first humans (Adam and Eve) chose to disobey and reject God. The Bible calls this sin. The consequence of sin is separation from God and death.

Ask: How would you describe sin?

Lead the kids to understand that disobedience and hurting others are sin. Guilt, shame, and blame are effects of sin that hurt our friendships with others—especially God. Being with God is the only way to be alive. Because of sin, we cannot be truly alive.

Explain: God wants to be with us. He likes us; we were made to be in relationship with Him. God wants us to enjoy the world He created and to live in good relationship with everyone around us. However, our sin and disobedience mean we can't be with God. We hurt our friends. We hurt the world.

Ask: Do you think you have ever disobeyed? Are you separated from God?

Ask: How can you be reunited with God?

Lead the children to see something must be done by God to reunite us with Him and to restore the world.

Read the Theme Verse:

Ephesians 2:8-10: "God saved you by his grace when you believed. And you can't take credit for this; it is a gift from God. Salvation is not a reward for the good things we have done, so none of us can boast about it. For we are God's masterpiece. He has created us anew in Christ Jesus, so we can do the good things he planned for us long ago."

Prayer:

Ask them to share things for which they want to pray. Pray as a group; encourage them to pray, as well.

Art Project: The Terrible Lie

Explain:
Using the Apple and Leaf Template, have the children cut out and glue the leaf to the apple. Next, cut on the dotted line to make a door in the heart. You may need to help younger students with this part.

On the outside of the door, write "The Terrible Lie." On the inside of the door, write: "You don't need God. You can be god on your own."

Supplies:
- Apple and Leaf Template (Download & print from: https://saturatetheworld.com/GB4K-extras)
- Crayons
- Scissors
- Pen

Week 3: Gospel Power

The Power of God to Save

Leader Preparation
Jesus Does it Better

The first-century church at Corinth had begun to question whether there was a bodily resurrection from the dead—whether people will be given new bodies to live in in a new world one day. This was huge! If people are not raised from the dead and given new bodies, then what happened with Jesus? Paul tells them our entire faith is futile if there is no resurrection (1 Corinthians 15:12–19). Paul confronted their wrong thinking by reminding them of the gospel.

If we have faith in Jesus to save us, we have been saved and are being saved.

Paul uses the language of being saved in describing what the gospel is still doing. Yes, the gospel is good news about a past event—Jesus lived and died at a definite time in history to forgive us of our sins. Yet the gospel is also good news about what God continues to do in us and through us. Jesus was raised from the dead on the third day. He is alive! He lives for us, and by His Spirit, He lives in us and works through us.

Most followers of Jesus believe that one day we will be like Him (1 John 3:2) and will live in a perfect world with Him. Many forget that in the present, He comes into our lives by His Spirit to give us a glimpse, a foretaste, of the future so we will live differently today. As we trust and depend on Him to work in us, He enables us to live the new and better life now.

Do you believe—or live as if—your holiness is enabled by your own power and strength? Do you truly believe the Spirit of God is alive and living in you today, and that He alone has the ability to work in and through you? If not, consider how this can be disbelief in what Jesus is currently doing in your life.

Suggested Lesson Outline

Here's a rough outline for this lesson. It's likely the story, craft, and prayer time will not fill all the time you have with the kids. This extra time is intentional. Free-play time is an important part of kids getting together!

Games, puzzles, or coloring sheets: 10-15 minutes
Get to know the name of each child. It's a good idea to have just a few things out instead of letting the kids get into anything they want in this time. For example, have out just puzzles, or use the coloring sheet for this lesson and have the kids start with coloring.

Review
During this time, engage the kids in what you talked about last week. You can ask the questions in the lesson and/or recite the summary paragraph in the lesson.

Story and discussion: 10 minutes
The story and discussion act like a script and are meant to be relational. They might take only five minutes; it depends on the children.

Theme verse and prayer: 5 minutes
Read the verse. You could ask the kids to stand and stretch, read the verse again, and then pray together.

Art time: 10-15 minutes
The art time is a great opportunity to go over the lesson again or hit points that you were not able to during the "sit down time." Place their art project and coloring sheet into their art box when they finish. At the end of the fourteen weeks, they will take their box home.

Group game/free play/singing: Remainder of time

> ### Extra Resources
> We've compiled videos, coloring sheets, and additional aids for this lesson and they're easy to use:
> https://saturatetheworld.com/GB4K-extras

Review

Teacher's Review: Last week's lesson was about the creation of the world. Adam and Eve had a good and rich life. We also talked about the separation caused by sin. In the previous week, they learned about God's character as being compassionate, merciful, gracious, and loving.

Explain: God is loving, compassionate, merciful, gracious, and forgiving. He shows us the best possible way to live in His world. He really loves us!

Ask: Do you remember what love means?

Say: All of this is who who God is; He is good.

Ask: What happened last week? How did God create the world? How did Adam and Eve live?

Ask: Do you remember what happened though? What is sin? What happens because of sin? What happens with us and God? Us and others?

Diving into Gospel Power

Explain: Remember, something must be done to make us alive again and in right relationship with God. Here's the good news: God so loved the world that He sent His only son, and whoever believes in Him will not die but live forever! (John 3:16).

Story: The Death of Jesus

You can pause throughout the story to ask clarifying questions or offer short explanations.

Many people welcomed Jesus, believing He was the King who would do the next great saving act of rescuing them. But, some of the religious leaders made a plan to murder Jesus. They conspired with Judas, one of Jesus's twelve disciples, about exactly how it would happen. They turned Jesus over to the Romans, calling Him a rebel. They demanded He, the one and true King of the earth, be beaten and killed—not just killed, but crucified. They hung him on a cross with nails—It was torture.

On a little hill outside Jerusalem, they crucified Jesus. The one and true King of the world was murdered. Hanging on a cross was the Messiah for whom many had been hoping, waiting, and longing. John looked on in horror. The King willingly hung on a cross and died . . . according to plan.

According to plan? Surely not! How could that be? Wasn't the plan that, as King, He would ascend to a throne and wear a crown of jewels? Wasn't the plan that every living creature would bow down before Him? The plan couldn't possibly have been Jesus hanging on a cross, wearing a crown of thorns, and having His enemies spit and curse at Him.

The one and true King was now the crucified and dead King. He had become a victim of the rebellion in the Garden of Eden, just like the rest of creation. He seemed no different.

However, God was still on His mission. The cross wasn't outside of God's plan to redeem and restore His creation. It was the white-hot center of it.

Three days later, some women went to the tomb where Jesus had been buried. He was gone! They went and told His disciples, who ran as fast as they could to the tomb. The disciples found it empty. Soon they would learn Jesus was indeed alive!

The crucified and dead King showed He absolutely was the one and true King. He did not succumb to the powers and effects of that original rebellion. He rose from the grave. He defeated death! He beat the curse!

Jesus was alive. The one and true King had defeated the enemies of the Kingdom decisively. A new day had dawned. What had been lost at Adam and Eve's sin in the Garden was now starting to be put right. Wow!

After reading the story, retell it in your own words. You can even ask for the kids to help you, too. As you retell this story, pause to ask them questions, such as: How does that make you feel? Why do you think Jesus did that?

Explain: Jesus came into our world and died for our sins. Jesus lived a life fully connected to God and without sin. He died for your sins. Remember: Sin separates us from God and causes death. Jesus became death for us, but God conquered death. He rose again! Because of Jesus, you are welcomed back into relationship, and He pursues you in relationship. You can not only be friends with God, but you can be His kids!

The Gospel is the power of God to save! WOW! Isn't that good news?

Ask: Why is that good news?

Explain: Remember, God is good. He gives us free gifts, and He is merciful. We were separated from God and were not the way we should be. Because God is so good, He sent His Son. If we believe in Him and repent of sin, we are free, alive, and with God! We are forgiven!

Ask: What do you think about that? Do you believe that?

Allow children to ask questions at this time. As kids ask questions, ask the class: Does anyone know the answer?

Review: What has Jesus done? Does God love us? How do we know God loves us?

Read the Theme Verse:

Ephesians 2:8-10: "God saved you by his grace when you believed. And you can't take credit for this; it is a gift from God. Salvation is not a reward for the good things we have done, so none of us can boast about it. For we are God's masterpiece. He has created us anew in Christ Jesus, so we can do the good things he planned for us long ago."

Prayer:

Invite the kids to pray, and ask the kids if there's anything they would like the rest of the group to pray about. Pray for the kids to understand and receive the love of God through the gospel.

Art Project: The Empty Cross

Directions:
Glue two popsicle sticks together to form a cross. Wrap the cloth around the cross as a fabric. (Purple is the color of royalty.) Use the pen to mark the nails for the hands and feet.

Supplies:
- Popsicle sticks
- Cloth scraps (preferably purple)
- Pen or marker

Week 4: Gospel Purpose

God is Making All Things New

Leader Preparation
Jesus Will Make it Better

What you love most, you also fear to lose the most. Whatever threatens what you love most controls you. We love God because He first loved us. He loved us by sending the Son to satisfy His just wrath against us for our sin. We have no need to fear judgment coming against us for our sin. Perfect love casts out fear (1 John 4:7–21).

First Peter 1:3–5 tells us that because of God's great mercy, "we have been born again, because God raised Jesus Christ from the dead. Now we live with great expectation, and we have a priceless inheritance—an inheritance that is kept in heaven for you, pure and undefiled, beyond the reach of change and decay. And through your faith, God is protecting you by his power until you receive this salvation, which is ready to be revealed on the last day for all to see." Not only do we have no need to be afraid of future judgment if our faith is in Jesus, but we also do not need to fear loss. Our salvation is kept in heaven for us. Also, Jesus is presently at the right hand of God the Father, representing all those who have faith in Him. He is securing us until the end, and He has all authority in heaven and on earth (Matthew 28:18). The thing that matters most cannot be taken away from us, and nothing can happen to prevent us from inheriting it.

Our relationship with God, our future salvation, and our hope to live eternally with Jesus on a new earth are already secured. If our faith is in Jesus to save us, we have been saved, we are being saved, and we will be saved.

Scripture also tells us that in the future, God will make all things new. All sin will be eradicated. All that is broken will be restored. Every person who belongs to Jesus will be healed. All relationships will be reconciled. We will enjoy a perfect world with Jesus at the center forever. It will be stunningly amazing! Jesus doesn't just hold and secure our future; He gives us a perfectly new one, as well.

Do you believe—or live as if—the future is unsure (even paralyzing)? Do you truly believe that eternity has been secured for you by the death and resurrection of Jesus? If not, how can this be understood as disbelief in what Jesus has promised to do?

Suggested Lesson Outline

Here's a rough outline for this lesson. It's likely the story, craft, and prayer time will not fill all the time you have with the kids. This extra time is intentional. Free-play time is an important part of kids getting together!

Games, puzzles, or coloring sheets: 10-15 minutes
Get to know the name of each child and build some foundational relationships. It's a good idea to have just a few things out instead of letting the kids get into anything they want in this time. For example, have out just puzzles, or use the coloring sheet for this lesson and have the kids start with coloring.

Review
During this time, engage the kids in what you talked about last week. You can ask the questions in the lesson and/or recite the summary paragraph in the lesson.

Story and discussion: 10 minutes
The story and discussion act like a script and are meant to be relational. They might take only five minutes; it depends on the children.

Theme verse and prayer: 5 minutes
Read the verse. You could ask the kids to stand and stretch, read the verse again, and then pray together.

Art time: 10-15 minutes
The art time is a great opportunity to go over the lesson again or hit points that you were not able to during the "sit down time." Place their art project and coloring sheet into their art box when they finish. At the end of the fourteen weeks, they will take their box home.

Group game/free play/singing: Remainder of time

> **Extra Resources**
> We've compiled videos, coloring sheets, and additional aids for this lesson and they're easy to use:
> https://saturatetheworld.com/GB4K-extras

Review

Teacher's Review: In the previous lessons, we learned about the character of God and His love for us. We talked about the power of God to bring salvation for sin through Jesus's love, life, death, and resurrection. This week's lesson is about the restoring purpose of the world for all things.

Explain: God is compassionate, merciful, gracious, forgiving, and loving. He really loves us!

Ask: Do you remember what forgiveness and compassion mean?

Ask: Do you remember what sin is? What happens because of sin? What happens with us and God? What about the relationship between us and others?

Ask: Do you remember that Jesus's death and His coming alive again mean you can have a good relationship with God?

Diving into Gospel Purpose

Explain: The good news about Jesus is not about you only. It's about the whole world. Not only is God making us new, but He is making the entire world new!

Story: Tell Everyone the Happy News

As you tell the story, pause to ask clarifying questions or offer short explanations. Help the kids imagine this moment..

After His death and resurrection, Jesus stayed on earth for forty days. During that time, Jesus gathered His followers back together. He began to show them from their history that what had happened to Him was all according to plan. God was still on a rescue mission, and He was sending them out to announce His reign to the world.

During those forty days, Jesus showed them His death and resurrection were needed to:

- Take the penalty for their sin on Himself.
- Defeat Satan.
- Redeem them from their slavery to sin.
- Secure the renewal of His creation.

Jesus's friends couldn't have been more excited. They were sitting in Jerusalem with Jesus, the one and true resurrected King. He was teaching them. He was about to take His throne and usher in the end of history. Finally, what they had been waiting, hoping, and longing for was here!

Not so fast. Jesus told Peter, John, and the others it was not yet time, and the story wasn't finished. More people still needed to hear this good news about the victorious King and His good Kingdom. It was not yet time for His Kingdom to come in full. Jesus's disciples learned that they and their friends were going to be sent out into the world as ambassadors.

Just as those angels had heralded the good news of Jesus's birth many years before . . .

Just as Jesus had heralded the news of His Kingdom and showed people what life is like in His Kingdom . . .

They, too, were going to be sent out to herald the good news of the true King's life, death, and resurrection. Together their lives and their voices would be a foretaste of and an invitation into the Kingdom life.

Before He ascended, Jesus told His disciples, "I am leaving you now, but I will come again one day. But for now, while you are here, I will send the Spirit of God to live in and among you. He will empower you for your mission to bring the good news of me and my Kingdom, making new disciples of me in every nation." Then He left, ascending to the right hand of the Father.

After reading the story, retell it in your own words, asking the children to help as you go.

Explain: God planned good things for us to do and ways for us to live as He has always wanted us to live. That's why He sent Christ to make us what we are—His masterpiece.

See, the story of Jesus is not just about us being made right with God, but also about us going into the world, having dinner with people, and showing them how God has changed us. It's about the world being made new! Our schools, our parks, our neighborhoods, and our cities need to be filled with the mercy, compassion, forgiveness, and love of God.

Ask: Why do you think God wants people to know the story of Jesus?

Ask: What do you think people need to know about Jesus?

Ask: What can you do to tell people about Jesus?

Ask: How can you show people what He is like?

READ THE THEME VERSE:

Ephesians 2:8-10: "God saved you by his grace when you believed. And you can't take credit for this; it is a gift from God. Salvation is not a reward for the good things we have done, so none of us can boast about it. For we are God's masterpiece. He has created us anew in Christ Jesus, so we can do the good things he planned for us long ago."

PRAYER:

Ask the kids if they know of people who do not know Jesus. Ask them if they want to pray for them to meet Jesus.

ART PROJECT: Megaphone

Explain:
You're creating a megaphone out of paper!

First, have the children decorate their piece of paper. When it is dry, roll and twist the paper into a cone. Tape or glue the cone together, and you have a megaphone to tell people the good news that Jesus is making all things new!

Supplies:
- White paper (card stock will work best)
- Stickers
- Markers or paint
- Staples, tape, or glue

Part 2

Our Gospel Identity

When we believe in Jesus, we are made new, given a new beginning and a new end.

Jesus said, "It is like we are born all over again!" (John 3:1-8)

Peter, one of Jesus's best friends, said, "We are born into a living hope!" (1 Peter 1:3)

This new life has nothing to do with what we have done or what we can do. It has everything to do with who God is, what He has done, and what He can do. In this section of the journey, we are going to cover a few changes in our identity and what it means to be "in Christ." Throughout this section, we'll remind the children and ourselves of God's character and the new identity we receive in Christ.

These four lessons can be summed up in what Paul wrote in 2 Corinthians 5:17: "This means that anyone who belongs to Christ has become a new person. The old life is gone; a new life has begun!"

Week 5: We are Disciples
Called to Learn from Jesus

Leaders Preparation
What is a Disciple?

When He called the first of His disciples, He said, "Come, follow me, and I will show you how to fish for people" (Matthew 4:19). They had been fishermen, but Jesus was calling them to fish for people. They responded by leaving everything—their families, their careers, their futures—to follow Jesus. It started in a boat and went out to the world. Those first disciples radically re-centered everything in their lives around Jesus, His teaching, and His mission. Their lives became all about Jesus! He was that important to them.

Then, after He had trained them for more than three years, suffered and died for their sins, and risen from the grave, Jesus told them to meet Him on a mountain before He ascended to heaven. On that mountain, He was going to give His final commission to them to make disciples of all people groups. Just as Jesus had called them to follow Him, be changed by Him, and obey Him, He sent them out to call others to follow Him, as well. He was going to send them to the ends of the earth so the world might be filled with the knowledge of God and the good news about Jesus.

They met Jesus on the mountain and worshiped Him there, but some still doubted (Matthew 28:16–17). They were in but not all in. Slow down, and don't miss this: Jesus's disciples had seen everything they needed to see. Jesus had taught them all He needed to teach them. They had experienced all they needed to experience with Jesus! Yet some were still doubting. This is good news for me! Though I've walked with Jesus for more than twenty-four years, I still struggle with doubts. Maybe you do, as well.

We're not alone! The disciples were still in-process—a process that would last their lifetimes. The same is true of us. That is what discipleship is all about. It is the ongoing process of submitting all of life to Jesus and seeing Him saturate your entire life and world with His presence and power. It's a process of growing daily in your awareness of your need for Him in the everyday stuff of life. It is walking with Jesus, being filled with Jesus, and being led by Jesus in every place and in every way.

Read the previous paragraph again. We hope it's a helpful definition of discipleship! How does that inform or challenge your view of discipleship?

Suggested Lesson Outline

Here's a rough outline for this lesson. It's likely the story, craft, and prayer time will not fill all the time you have with the kids. This extra time is intentional. Free-play time is an important part of kids getting together!

Games, puzzles, or coloring sheets: 10-15 minutes
Get to know the name of each child and build some foundational relationships. It's a good idea to have just a few things out instead of letting the kids get into anything they want in this time. For example, have out just puzzles, or use the coloring sheet for this lesson and have the kids start with coloring.

Review
During this time, engage the kids in what you talked about last week. You can ask the questions in the lesson and/or recite the summary paragraph in the lesson.

Story and discussion: 10 minutes
The story and discussion act like a script and are meant to be relational. They might take only five minutes; it depends on the children.

Theme verse and prayer: 5 minutes
Read the verse. You could ask the kids to stand and stretch, read the verse again, and then pray together.

Art time: 10-15 minutes
The art time is a great opportunity to go over the lesson again or hit points that you were not able to during the "sit down time." Place their art project and coloring sheet into their art box when they finish. At the end of the fourteen weeks, they will take their box home.

Group game/free play/singing: Remainder of time

> ### Extra Resources
> We've compiled videos, coloring sheets, and additional aids for this lesson and they're easy to use:
> **https://saturatetheworld.com/GB4K-extras**

Review

Remind the kids of the last four weeks, when they learned about who God is and what He has done in Jesus to bring us back into relationship with Him and how God is restoring the world that was broken through Jesus's life, death, and resurrection.

Last week's lesson was about how Jesus rose from the dead, but the story doesn't end there! Now we're part of His rescue mission!

Ask: What do you remember about the gospel story?

Diving into Gospel Identity

Explain: When we believe in Jesus, we are made new, given a new beginning and a new end.

Jesus said, "It is like we are born all over again!"

Peter, one of Jesus's best friends, said, "We are born into a living hope!"

This new life has nothing to do with what we have done or what we can do. It has everything to do with who God is, what He has done, and what He can do.

Story #1: Jesus Asks People to Follow Him[1]

As you read the story, pause to ask clarifying questions or offer short explanations to engage the kids.

One day as Jesus was walking along the shore of the Sea of Galilee, He saw Simon and his brother Andrew throwing a net into the water, for they fished for a living. Jesus called out to them, "Come, follow me, and I will show you how to fish for people!" And they left their nets at once and followed Him.

A little farther up the shore, Jesus saw Zebedee's sons, James and John, in a boat repairing their nets. He called them at once, and they also followed Him, leaving their father, Zebedee, in the boat with the hired men.

---

[1] This week's story is directly from Matthew 4:18-22, New Living Translation, except for parenthesis which are added to give children clarity.

Explain: Jesus told them, "Come and follow me, and I will teach you a whole new way of living!" They were ordinary people (they all had problems) who dropped everything to listen to Jesus, ask Him questions, and see how He lived—then He helped them live that way, too!

Ask: How do you learn new things?

Consider asking the kids to explain how they have learned to ride a bike, play soccer, build Legos, sing a song, etc.

Ask: How do you think Jesus teaches us a whole new way of living?

Story #2: Zacchaeus[2]

Pause throughout the story to ask clarifying questions or offer simple explanations.

Jesus entered Jericho (a big city) and made His way through the town. There was a man there named Zacchaeus. He was the chief tax collector (someone who was a bully and betrayed many people) in the region, and he had become very rich. He tried to get a look at Jesus, but he was too short to see over the crowd. He ran ahead and climbed a sycamore-fig tree beside the road because Jesus was going to pass that way.

When Jesus came by, He looked up at Zacchaeus and called him by name. "Zacchaeus!" He said. "Quick, come down! I must be a guest in your home today."

Zacchaeus quickly climbed down and took Jesus to his house in great excitement and joy. But the people were displeased. "He has gone to be the guest of a notorious sinner," they grumbled.

Meanwhile, Zacchaeus stood before the Lord and said, "I will give half my wealth to the poor, Lord, and if I have cheated people on their taxes, I will give them back four times as much!"

Jesus responded, "Today, salvation has come to this house!"

---

[2] This week's story is directly from Luke 19:1-9, New Living Translation, except for parenthesis which are added to give children clarity.

After this story, ask the kids to retell what happened. You can help them along as they do.

Ask: What changed for Zacchaeus? How did he change?

Ask: How good do you have to be to start following Jesus?

Jesus only asks you to come and follow. It doesn't matter how good you are, how smart you are, what your grades are, how nice your clothes are, or where you live.

Explain: As Jesus walked on the earth, more and more people began to follow Him, and more and more began to model their lives after Him. They helped Jesus feed people, heal people, and teach people.

Jesus not only taught them new things in their brains, but He changed their hearts—what they believed. Not only did their hearts and brains change, the way they did everything changed, too.

When we believe in Jesus and begin to follow Him, we become that kind of student. Jesus is our teacher in everything and in every part of our lives.

Ask: What does it mean to be a "student of Jesus"? What changes?

Ask: How do we learn from Jesus?

Explain: Jesus invites us to listen to, learn from, and follow Him in everything—not just learning facts or test questions or schoolwork, but learning how to treat other people and love others as He loves us.

We are learning about Jesus with our heads (our brains/thoughts), our hearts (our feelings/emotions), and our hands (what we do/how we live).

Read the Theme Verse:

2 Corinthians 5:17: "This means that anyone who belongs to Christ has become a new person. The old life is gone; a new life has begun!"

Prayer:

Ask the kids if there is anything they want to pray for. Let them pray for each other. As the leader, pray last in light of today's lesson.

Art Project: New Life Butterfly

Directions:

You're creating a butterfly! Explain how butterflies first are caterpillars and then transform into something completely new—like we are when we find our identity in Jesus! Have the kids cut out the butterfly pattern (or adults do ahead of time) and color the body. Next, they will cut the tissue paper into small pieces, and glue them on the wings of the butterfly. This will create a beautiful and colorful piece of artwork.

Supplies:
- Butterfly pattern (Download & print from: https://saturatetheworld.com/GB4K-extras)
- Colorful tissue paper
- Glue
- Markers or crayons

Week 6: We are Family

The Father Has Adopted Us as Children of God

Leaders Preparation
Adopted Child of God

Read: Romans 8:15–17

When the Holy Spirit takes up residence in our lives, we, too, can cry, "Abba, Father." The same Spirit that proceeds from the relationship between the Father and Son implants in us. The difference between Jesus and us is that He is the natural Son of the Father, whereas we are adopted into the family through His sacrifice.

We are all spiritual orphans. Our rebellious and sinful nature cut us off from God the Father. The Bible says quite clearly we are not born children of God and therefore must go through an adoption process. The price of our adoption was the death of God's Son. C.S. Lewis wrote, "The Son of God became a man to enable men to become the sons of God." [3]

The good news is that when we recognize we are spiritual orphans in need of the Father, we can go through the Son. When we acknowledge that our sin has severed the relationship with the Father and that Jesus is the gracious payment for our sin, and when we then accept the gift of forgiveness offered by inviting the Spirit of Jesus into our life, then we can cry, "Abba, Father." We are at home, at last, welcomed into God's family.

As adopted children, we can enjoy the same favor Jesus has with the Father. We, too, are the apple of God's eye, the pleasure of His love, the delight of His focus. If we didn't get all we wanted or needed in our human fathers, we are invited even more deeply into the pleasure that the Father of heaven and earth takes in His Son and us. We have been included in the family and hear the Father say, "You are my child, whom I love; with you I am well pleased." We now have the Father we always needed and wanted.

Our Rich Inheritance

But that's not where the text ends. If we are full-fledged members of the family, an inheritance is waiting for us. "And since we are his children, we are his heirs. In fact, together with Christ, we are heirs of God's glory" (Romans 8:17a). We have been included in the will and stand to inherit such things as resurrection bodies that do not decay, a new heaven, and a new earth, for starters. The will also mentions we'll have a family to spend eternity with, in a life free of pain, crying, disease, and death. However, that's still not the best part. The best part is that we are heirs of God.

The best part is that we are heirs of God. They will reads, "I, God, bequeath myself to you for all eternity."

We are heirs of God and coheirs with Christ, and therefore we get in on all Jesus inherits. When Jesus was in the upper room before going to the cross, He longed to return to the presence of His Father. He prayed in John 17:5, "Now, Father, bring me into the glory we shared before the world began."

Jesus was looking forward to the joy on the other side of the cross. The writer of Hebrews says that "Because of the joy awaiting him, he endured the cross, disregarding its shame" (Hebrews 12:2). As coheirs with Jesus, we get to share in the glory the Father bestows on the Son. As Jesus prayed moments before His arrest, He made our inheritance with Him plain: "Father, I want these whom you have given me to be with me where I am. Then they can see all the glory you gave me because you loved me even before the world began" (John 17:24). Jesus wraps up His prayer by asking the Father to bestow on us the same love He has for Jesus: "I have revealed you to them, and I will continue to do so. Then your love for me will be in them, and I will be in them" (John 17:26).

We are drawn into the family circle and get to enjoy the spillover of the Father's love for the Son. As we bring this section on the message of Christ to a close, we end where we started. We began examining the meaning of being created in the image of God and discovered this meant we were created for relationship. To be adopted into God's family is to be restored to paradise lost. God sent Jesus as the image of the invisible God (Colossians 1:15) to restore the image of God in us. We find our way home only when the Holy Spirit comes to take residence in us, and we cry out, "Abba, Father." Welcome home!

When are times you have seen a small child cry, "Dada"? (Abba means Dada.) Why does a child call for a parent in his or her time of need?

Do you ever call God "Dad" in prayer? If not, how might your times in prayer change if you called God "Dad" instead of simply "Lord" or "God"?

What is an heir? How is being an heir better than being a slave?

---

[3] C.S. Lewis, quoted in Hymns for the Family of God (Nashville: Paragon, 1976), p. 167.

Suggested Lesson Outline

Here's a rough outline for this lesson. It's likely the story, craft, and prayer time will not fill all the time you have with the kids. This extra time is intentional. Free-play time is an important part of kids getting together!

Games, puzzles, or coloring sheets: 10-15 minutes
Get to know the name of each child and build some foundational relationships. It's a good idea to have just a few things out instead of letting the kids get into anything they want in this time. For example, have out just puzzles, or use the coloring sheet for this lesson and have the kids start with coloring.

Review
During this time, engage the kids in what you talked about last week. You can ask the questions in the lesson and/or recite the summary paragraph in the lesson.

Story and discussion: 10 minutes
The story and discussion act like a script and are meant to be relational. They might take only five minutes; it depends on the children.

Theme verse and prayer: 5 minutes
Read the verse. You could ask the kids to stand and stretch, read the verse again, and then pray together.

Art time: 10-15 minutes
The art time is a great opportunity to go over the lesson again or hit points that you were not able to during the "sit down time." Place their art project and coloring sheet into their art box when they finish. At the end of the fourteen weeks, they will take their box home.

Group game/free play/singing: Remainder of time

> ### Extra Resources
> We've compiled videos, coloring sheets, and additional aids for this lesson and they're easy to use:
> https://saturatetheworld.com/GB4K-extras

REVIEW

In last week's lesson, the kids heard the story of Jesus calling the disciples to follow him and Zacchaeus. The kids discussed how believing in Jesus means we learn for the rest of our lives how to follow him. Not only that, but we're made new!

Ask: What do you remember about last week?

Remind the kids that when you believe in Jesus, you change, and God changes you. You have a whole new identity!

Diving into Family Identity

Explain: When you believe in God, it means you are part of a new family—actually a really BIG family.

Way back in the old days, God had a close friend, whose name was Abraham. The following is a story about him and the family of God.

STORY: God's Family "Project"

As you read the story, feel free to pause and offer short explanations.

After Adam and Eve sinned in the garden, things got really out of hand. Brothers killed each other, people stole and lied, and everyone did terrible things. Was God going to give up on the world? Could He really continue to allow humans to destroy the beautiful world He created? No!

God had a plan. He wouldn't walk away from His creation and from the people who were made in His image. Instead, He chose a man, Abraham, and his wife, Sarah, to become His special family. Wait, God's big plan was a family? Yes! See, God promised them He would make them into a big family. They would have so many kids and so many grandkids and so many great-grandkids, and so many great-great-grandkids that their offspring would be like the stars—more than you could count. What was God going to do through this family?

First, they were going to be God's family. He was going to be the one who provided for, cared for, and walked with them. They were His people, and He would never forget about them.

Second, He was going to bless the world through them. This family, because they were God's family, was going to show the world exactly what God was like: good, gracious, compassionate, forgiving, and, above all, loving!

Guess what? That family didn't do so well in showing the world what God was like. They didn't bless the world. In fact, they looked a lot like all the other families in the world: selfish, bitter, and far from God.

However, God never gave up on them. In fact, guess who Abraham and Sarah's great-great-great-great-great-great-great-great-grandson was? Jesus. Jesus came into the world as the blessing to the world that Abraham and His family never were. Then, through the power of the gospel, Jesus's family grows, and anyone who is with Jesus is a member of God's family.

Ask: Through whom was God going to change the world? Lead the kids to see it was through a family.

Ask: What would this family do for everyone on the earth? Lead the kids to see it was to be a blessing.

Ask: What is God's family like? They are a blessing. They are special and in relationship with God. They get to have a blessed, dream-come-true kind of life!

Explain: When you believe, you are adopted into this big family—a family that blesses the world! One of Jesus' good friends, John, once said, "See how very much our Father loves us, for he calls us his children, and that is what we are" (1 John 3:1a). See, you are God's child.

Ask: If we are God's family, what does that mean about us?

Explain: God deeply loves us, and He is our Father. It means we love one another and show the world what God is like by how we love Him and others.

Read the Theme Verse:

2 Corinthians 5:17: "This means that anyone who belongs to Christ has become a new person. The old life is gone; a new life has begun!"

Prayer:

Ask the kids if there is anything for which they want to pray. Let them pray for each other. As the leader, pray last in light of today's lesson.

Art Project: God's Family Tree

Directions:

They will make their family tree, but not their biological family tree—the tree of the family of God. In each circle for a "family member," encourage them to draw the picture (stick-figure) or face of someone in God's family. Have them think about each other! They can also include characters from the Bible or others in their community.

Supplies:

- Family tree template (Download & print from: https://saturatetheworld.com/GB4K-extras)
- Markers or crayons

Week 7: We are Servants
Jesus Served, and Jesus is King

Leaders Preparation
The King, His Kingdom, & His Servants

Jesus claimed to be a king and not just any king. He claimed to be the King over all kings—God Himself. However, Jesus gave us an atypical picture of kingship. When two of Jesus's disciples were arguing about who would be higher in His kingdom, He said to them in Mark 10:42a–45:

". . . You know that the rulers in this world lord it over their people, and officials flaunt their authority over those under them. But among you it will be different. Whoever wants to be a leader among you must be your servant, and whoever wants to be first among you must be the slave of everyone else. For even the Son of Man came not to be served but to serve others and to give his life as a ransom for many."

Much of the Christian life sounds more exciting than serving others. Meditation on Scripture appeals to our desire for spiritual depth. Fasting can strike us as a challenge to rugged, self-denying discipleship. But serving? It sounds mundane, even demeaning.

Enter Jesus and the gospel. Jesus declared, "For even the Son of Man came not to be served but to serve others and to give his life as a ransom for many" (Matthew 20:28). God works through the gospel of Jesus in part to make people like Jesus. As Jesus came not to be served but instead as one who had the heart of a servant, so those who believe the gospel of Jesus are given Christ-like hearts of servants.

The gospel of Jesus Christ transforms enemies of God into servants of God. The Holy Spirit still works through the gospel to turn those who serve their idols (such as wealth, careers, sports, sex, houses, land, and so on) into servants of God. The Holy Spirit does this as He did in the apostle Paul's day when the missionary wrote to some relatively new Christians that they "turned away from idols to serve the living and true God" (1 Thessalonians 1:9b).

One way the gospel turns sinners into servants is by humbling their pride. Through the gospel, people see God is holy and that each of us deserves His wrath for breaking His law an infinite number of times. The gospel shows us what Christ did for sinners and how blessed we are to be received into His Kingdom and family. As a result of understanding this incomparable message and experiencing God through it, people willingly serve Him and His gospel.

One of the clearest indications that people have believed the gospel of Jesus is that their selfish desires to be served begin to be overcome by a Christ-like desire to serve. They start looking for ways to do something for Christ's church, especially in ways that will serve the gospel.

The transformation in people's nature that God effects through the gospel also turns selfish people—interested only in serving themselves and being served by others—into people who, in the words of the apostle Peter, want to "serve one another" (1 Peter 4:10). The gospel opens believers' eyes to see needs they never saw before and changes their hearts to have a new compassion and willingness to meet those needs.

As the Holy Spirit permeates people's character with the effects of the gospel, they increasingly develop a mindset of serving in every part of life. They begin to consider their daily occupation in terms of how useful it should be in the service of others instead of simply how it enlarges their wealth or reputation. They give more thought to serving the members of their families. They want to know their churches are stronger because of their service.

If you are a Christian, you have been purchased by Jesus and are no longer a slave to sin but are now a servant of Jesus. Why is it good news that we are servants of Jesus? How do we know He is a better master than sin?

Suggested Lesson Outline

Here's a rough outline for this lesson. It's likely the story, craft, and prayer time will not fill all the time you have with the kids. This extra time is intentional. Free-play time is an important part of kids getting together!

Games, puzzles, or coloring sheets: 10-15 minutes
Get to know the name of each child and build some foundational relationships. It's a good idea to have just a few things out instead of letting the kids get into anything they want in this time. For example, have out just puzzles, or use the coloring sheet for this lesson and have the kids start with coloring.

Review
During this time, engage the kids in what you talked about last week. You can ask the questions in the lesson and/or recite the summary paragraph in the lesson.

Story and discussion: 10 minutes
The story and discussion act like a script and are meant to be relational. They might take only five minutes; it depends on the children.

Theme verse and prayer: 5 minutes
Read the verse. You could ask the kids to stand and stretch, read the verse again, and then pray together.

Art time: 10-15 minutes
The art time is a great opportunity to go over the lesson again or hit points that you were not able to during the "sit down time." Place their art project and coloring sheet into their art box when they finish. At the end of the fourteen weeks, they will take their box home.

Group game/free play/singing: Remainder of time

> ### Extra Resources
> We've compiled videos, coloring sheets, and additional aids for this lesson and they're easy to use:
> https://saturatetheworld.com/GB4K-extras

Review

Teacher's Review: Last week's lesson was about how God chose Abraham's family to be a blessing to the world. God wanted to use family to heal, restore, and show the world what God is really like. While Abraham and his family didn't do that well, God hasn't given up on using Family to change the world. When we believe in Jesus we become part of His family—the Church. Two lessons ago, the children learned that following Jesus means a new identity—a life of learning to follow Jesus.

Ask: What happens when we believe in Jesus? Do we change? How do we change?

Ask: What does it mean to be a student of Jesus?

Ask: What does it mean to be a son or daughter of God?

Remind them that because God is a good Father, we have been given every blessing as His kids! We also get to follow Him and learn how to love God as His disciples.

Diving into Servant Identity

Explain: When we believe in Jesus, we are made new and given a new beginning and a new end. Jesus said, "It is like we are born all over again!" Peter (one of Jesus's best friends) said, "We are born into hope!"

This new life has nothing to do with what we have done or what we can do. It has everything to do with who God is, what He has done, and what He can do. In this section of the journey, we are going to cover a few changes in our identity and what it means to be "in Christ."

Today, we are going to see how Jesus has made us servants.

Ask: What do you think a servant is?

Ask: Why do you think we become servants?

STORY: The Servant King[4]

As you tell the story, pause throughout to ask clarifying questions or offer short explanations.

Before the Passover celebration (a big and important meal), Jesus knew His hour had come to leave this world and return to His Father. He had loved His disciples during His ministry on earth, and now He loved them to the very end. Jesus knew that the Father had given Him authority over everything and that He had come from God and would return to God. (Wow, He had authority or control or ownership over everything! Basically, He was King of the world!) So He got up from the table, took off His robe, wrapped a towel around His waist, and poured water into a basin. Then He began to wash the disciples' feet, drying them with the towel He had around Him. (The king served?)

Then later he said: "And since I, your King and Teacher, have washed your feet, you should wash each other's feet. I have given you an example to follow. Do what I have done."

Earlier in His life, Jesus told His disciples, "Even though I'm God's Son, I didn't come to be served but to serve others and to give my life for many." (He meant He would serve and die for other people.)

Retell the story.

Ask: Why and how was Jesus a servant? How did He serve others?

Lead the kids to see that Jesus was a servant. He helped people who could not help themselves. He was humble, and He cared for people. You can also point to the story of Jesus feeding thousands of people or healing people. Ultimately lead the kids to the fact that Jesus died for other people. Allow them to share stories.

Ask: What does it mean that Jesus is the King?

Ask: Do you remember what He said at the end of today's story?

Explain: He said to do this for each other. He makes us servants, just like Him!

Because Christ first loved us and because Jesus serves us, Jesus is the King, and we are His servants, helping Him love the world. We belong to King Jesus.

---

[4] This week's story is directly from John 13:1, 3-5, 14-15, New Living Translation, except for parenthesis which are added to give children clarity.

Ask/Activity: What can you do this week to serve Jesus?

Help the kids brainstorm how they can help a friend, neighbor, parent, or sibling. After each kid comes up with an idea (ideas are contagious, and kids often pick the same things), have them draw a picture or work with them to write a note that would remind them to serve others as a way to serve Jesus as King.

Read the Theme Verse:

2 Corinthians 5:17: "This means that anyone who belongs to Christ has become a new person. The old life is gone; a new life has begun!"

Prayer:

Ask the kids if there is anything they want to pray for. Let them pray for that. As a leader, pray over the kids that they can be servants and that they would submit their whole lives to Jesus.

Art Project: Crown of Christ

Directions:

Make a crown out of paper and decorate it. First, have the children decorate their strips with jewels and other decorative features. Then curve the strips into headbands and staple both ends together. Lead the kids to remember Jesus is the King of everything, yet He served and called us to be servants, too. Our King and Master is Jesus!

Supplies:

- Strips of construction paper to be made into crowns
- Glue
- Scissors
- Stapler
- Jewel stickers (You can find these at most craft stores.)

Week 8:
We are Missionaries
The Holy Spirit Empowers Us as Witnesses

Leader Preparation
Always on Mission

This is the last of three weeks in which we're considering our gospel identities. As a reminder, our identity informs everything we do, and our identity is founded on who God is and His work in us. Because of the gospel, our new identities are as family, servants, and missionaries. Two weeks ago, we talked about family. Last week we considered servants, and this week we wrap up our identity conversations by considering our missionary identity.

We are missionaries empowered by the Holy Spirit. We follow the leading of the Spirit as we show and share the good news of Jesus.

If you're a follower of Jesus who believes the gospel is the central motivation in your life, then your first priority in life is to live as a disciple who makes disciples. This means more than just "making converts." It means living out your everyday life and rhythms in a way that encourages other followers of Jesus in areas of their lives where they don't functionally live out God's gospel story. It also means living out your everyday life and rhythms in a way that introduces not-yet believers to God's gospel story in real, tangible ways. That's part of "the good things [God] planned for us long ago" (Ephesians 2:10) and "His work" your leaders equip you for (Ephesians 4:12). Read Jesus's own words to His followers: "As the Father has sent me, so I am sending you" (John 20:21b).

Remember, you are not alone on this mission. Jesus goes with you everywhere because His Spirit is in you to empower you to be His representative in the world. He wants to saturate your world in word and deed by His presence at work in and through you by His Spirit.

We are the Father's family; therefore, we love others just as He loved us.

We are servants of Christ; therefore, we serve the least of these as He served us.

We are missionaries led and empowered by the same Spirit that was in Jesus; therefore, we are always on-mission to proclaim the good news of Jesus.

Whatever He has done to us, He now wants to do through us.

To whom is God calling you to be a missionary? How are you seeing your identity shaped and remade by God?

Suggested Lesson Outline

Here's a rough outline for this lesson. It's likely the story, craft, and prayer time will not fill all the time you have with the kids. This extra time is intentional. Free-play time is an important part of kids getting together!

Games, puzzles, or coloring sheets: 10-15 minutes
Get to know the name of each child and build some foundational relationships. It's a good idea to have just a few things out instead of letting the kids get into anything they want in this time. For example, have out just puzzles, or use the coloring sheet for this lesson and have the kids start with coloring.

Review
During this time, engage the kids in what you talked about last week. You can ask the questions in the lesson and/or recite the summary paragraph in the lesson.

Story and discussion: 10 minutes
The story and discussion act like a script and are meant to be relational. They might take only five minutes; it depends on the children.

Theme verse and prayer: 5 minutes
Read the verse. You could ask the kids to stand and stretch, read the verse again, and then pray together.

Activity: 10-15 minutes
The activity is a great time to go over the lesson again or hit points that you were not able to during the "sit down time."

Group game/free play/singing: Remainder of time

> **Extra Resources**
> We've compiled videos, coloring sheets, and additional aids for this lesson and they're easy to use:
> https://saturatetheworld.com/GB4K-extras

Review

Teacher's review: Last week the kids learned about Jesus being the King of the world and His people being servants. The story was about Jesus washing the disciples' feet and how all his disciples are called to be servants: to Jesus and to others.

Ask: What did Jesus do on earth?

Explain: Jesus told people about the best type of living. He spent time with them, healed sick people, forgave people's sins, served people, died on the cross for everyone's sin, and rose again! Death did not win—Jesus did!

Diving into Missionary Identity:

Ask: What do you think the last thing Jesus said was? Let the kids guess.

Story: "Be My Witnesses"[5]

As you tell the story, pause throughout to ask clarifying questions or offer short explanations.

When the apostles were with Jesus, they kept asking Him, "Lord, has the time come for you to free Israel and restore our kingdom?" (They wanted to know when everything would be made right and they could live with Jesus forever.)

He replied, "The Father alone has the authority to set those dates and times, and they are not for you to know. (Jesus is already King, and we don't need to know when.) But you will receive power when the Holy Spirit comes upon you. And you will be my witnesses (or missionaries), telling people about me everywhere—in Jerusalem, throughout Judea, in Samaria, and to the ends of the earth. (That's their city, their state, their country, and their planet)."

Jesus also told the people who were following Him, "Go and tell everyone in the world about me, help them follow me, and baptize them in the name of the Father and the Son and the Holy Spirit. Teach these new followers how to obey all the commands I have given you."

---

[5] This week's story is directly from Acts 1:6-8, New Living Translation, except for parenthesis which are added to give children clarity.

Explain: Those are the last words of Jesus!

Do you know what this is? If you believe in Jesus, this is your job description. This is who you are and what Jesus has told you to do. It's like you're a commercial for Jesus and His Kingdom.

Read: Reread the verses and ask the kids to list what they should do: "Go and tell everyone in the world about me, help them follow me, and baptize them in the name of the Father and the Son and the Holy Spirit. Teach these new followers how to obey all the commands I have given you."

Ask: What is our job description?
1) Go and tell everyone about Jesus.
2) Help them follow Jesus.
3) Baptize them. (Ask the kids what baptism is.)
4) Teach them how to obey the command He has given us.

Explain: The Bible says when you believe in Jesus and follow Jesus, you become someone who goes and tells people about Jesus. Often, believers were called "sent ones" or "missionaries." If you follow Jesus, you are a missionary, doing the stuff Jesus did on earth!

Ask: How can you tell people about Jesus?

Ask: Who can you tell about Jesus?

Ask: How can you teach them what it means to obey Jesus?

Read the Theme Verse:

2 Corinthians 5:17: "This means that anyone who belongs to Christ has become a new person. The old life is gone; a new life has begun!"

Prayer:

Ask the kids if there is anything for which they want to pray.

Activity: Movement Tag

Directions:

Two people are "it" as disciples to start the game and must link arms or hold hands as they try to tag others. Each time they tag someone, that person joins the "movement" and links arms with them.

At any given time, the leader can yell, "Scatter," which means the movement breaks up, and they can begin trying to tag each other and build a "movement" again.

Part 3
Gospel Life

We have learned about who God is and what He has done for us. We have also learned about how God changes us and makes us new people. Now we are going to talk about how we live and what we do differently because of Jesus.

To lead our children to see all of life as ministry and mission, we must equip them to live out the gospel in everyday activities—everyday rhythms. We have found some transferable patterns or rhythms of life that we see throughout "The Story of God" and in every culture in every part of the world.[6] Through each of these rhythms, people have the opportunity to walk by faith (walking in line with the truth of the gospel) or walk in fear or prideful rebellion to God (walking in unbelief).

Theme Verse for Gospel Life:

Ephesians 4:1 says, "Therefore . . . lead a life worthy of your calling, for you have been called by God. "

---

[6] *The Story of God for Kids* is another foundational resource for children in missional churches.

Week 1: Listen

We Pray to Jesus and Listen to Others

Leader Preparation
Everyday Listening

Everybody is listening all the time. Who or what are we listening to, and are we paying attention to what we're hearing? "Listening" means that we pay careful attention to God and others. By knowing God's story, setting aside time to listen to God's voice above others, and listening well to our family and mission field, we speak the greater truth of God's story and work on areas of disbelief—ours and "theirs"—by comparing those other, lesser stories to Jesus's greater one.

We listen to God: As God's people, we have His Spirit in us, regularly speaking to us through the Scriptures as we read them and recall them. Through His church, we interact with one another, and personally, we listen closely to His voice. (In John 10:1–21, Jesus said His sheep hear and listen to His voice, and in John 14–15, He said His Spirit would be the means by which we abide with Him and are led by Him.) Listening also reminds us that the Spirit can speak to others in our silence. In fact, our willingness to quiet our souls and care for others often creates the best space for the Spirit to work. One of Jesus's titles is "Wonderful Counselor" (Isaiah 9:6). He said that when He left He would send "another Counselor" (John 14:16, RSV), the Holy Spirit, to come and dwell in us. If you are a child of God, you have the Counselor living in you.

We listen to others: People are interesting. If we listen, we will discover this. They are image-bearers of God. They are broken, marred, and not fully together, just like we are—but they are image-bearers nonetheless. It's incredible, when you take the time to listen, how much you can learn. You begin to see how amazingly unique and creative each one of God's image-bearers is. One of the greatest gifts we can give one another is a set of open ears and a closed mouth. Sure, there are times to speak, but are we willing to listen to one another?

We set aside regular times to listen to God both "backward" and "forward." Jesus listened to God in prayer to know His Father's will. We are also called to listen to God. We listen "backward" by regularly interacting with God's Word—the Story and the Son. We also believe He speaks today through His Spirit in us and through creation. We spend time actively listening "forward" to hear what God is saying to us today (Mark 1:35–37; John 16:7–15; Hebrews 1:1–3; Romans 1:20).

How do you struggle to listen to others and God? How does your identity in Christ challenge the way you listen and to whom you listen?

Suggested Lesson Outline

Here's a rough outline for this lesson. It's likely the story, craft, and prayer time will not fill all the time you have with the kids. This extra time is intentional. Free-play time is an important part of kids getting together!

Games, puzzles, or coloring sheets: 10-15 minutes
Get to know the name of each child and build some foundational relationship. It's a good idea to have just a few things out instead of letting the kids get into anything they want in this time. For example, have out just puzzles, or use the coloring sheet for this lesson and have the kids start with coloring.

Review
During this time, engage the kids in what you talked about last week. You can ask the questions in the lesson and/or recite the summary paragraph in the lesson.

Story and discussion: 10 minutes
The story and discussion act like a script and are meant to be relational. They might take only five minutes; it depends on the children.

Theme verse and prayer: 5 minutes
Read the verse. You could ask the kids to stand and stretch, read the verse again, and then pray together.

Activity: The game "Telephone" 5-10 minutes

Art time: 10-15 minutes
The art time is a great opportunity to go over the lesson again or hit points that you were not able to during the "sit down time." Place their art project and coloring sheet into their art box when they finish. At the end of the fourteen weeks, they will take their box home.

Group game/free play/singing: Remainder of time

> ### Extra Resources
> We've compiled videos, coloring sheets, and additional aids for this lesson and they're easy to use:
> https://saturatetheworld.com/GB4K-extras

Review

Teacher's Review: The previous section of this curriculum was about our gospel identity as disciples who are family, servants, and missionaries. This is who we are because God is a Father who has adopted us as sons and daughters. Jesus is the servant King who welcomes us into His kingdom as servants. And the Holy Spirit empowers us to be witnesses and tell the world what God is like and what He has done.

Ask: Do you remember who we are?

You may need to remind them we are children of the Father, servants to Jesus, and missionaries empowered by the Spirit.

Explain: So far, we have learned about who God is and what He has done for us. We have also learned about how God changes us and makes us new people. Now we are going to talk about how we live and what we do differently because of Jesus. Actually, it's not so much that we do extra things, but that Jesus changes how we do them!

Diving into the Rhythm of Listening

Explain: The first thing that changes is how we listen!

Ask: What does it mean to listen?

Story : "Teach Us to Pray"

Luke 16, Luke 18, and Matthew 6

As you tell the story, you may pause to ask clarifying questions or offer short explanations to keep them engaged.

Jesus was often listening to the Father. His disciples saw Him praying all the time, so one day when Jesus finished praying and listening to God, His disciples came to Him and asked, "Lord, teach us to pray, just as John taught his disciples."

Jesus said, "This is how you should pray: 'Father, may your name be kept holy. May your Kingdom come soon. Give us each day the food we need, and forgive us our sins. Help us forgive people who sin against us. Help us stop sinning.'"

Sometimes people would be proud and want to be noticed, so they would pray: "I thank you, God, that I am not like other people—cheaters, sinners, and bad people. I'm certainly not like those other people! I do everything right!" They used big words, and they were trying to prove themselves to God.

However, Jesus taught them, "When you pray, don't be like those people who love to pray publicly on street corners and in church where everyone can see them. When you pray, go away by yourself, shut the door behind you, and pray to your Father in private. Pray like you're talking to your daddy— because you are."

Ask:	How should we pray? (in a normal voice, like you're talking to someone)
Ask:	Why does God listen to us?
Explain:	He loves us! He enjoys us. He is our Dad!
Ask:	What did Jesus pray for? (You may have to read the beginning of the story again.)
Explain:	He prayed to be close to God and for God to make things right. He prayed for God to give us what we need, to forgive us, to help us forgive, and to keep us safe, and Jesus acknowledges that God is in charge! This is how we should pray.
Ask:	Why should we pray?
Explain:	Not only does God hear us, but God speaks to us.
Ask:	What does God say? How does He talk to us?
Explain:	We believe Jesus loves us and listens to us. Not only that, but He speaks to us. We pray and read the Bible to know who God is and what He does. That is why we listen to God. Every time we read the Bible or hear the Story of God, He is speaking to us! We also hear Him when we pray.
Ask:	Have you ever tried to be really, really still and listen?
Ask:	If someone is going to tell you something important, how do you make sure you will hear?

Read the Theme Verse:

Ephesians 4:1 says, "Therefore . . . lead a life worthy of your calling, for you have been called by God."

Prayer:

Ask the kids if there is anything they want to pray for. Let them pray for each other. As the leader, pray last in light of today's lesson.

Activity: "Telephone"

Have kids sit or stand in a circle or a line. Play the game "Telephone," where the kids relay a message from one kid to the next, until the same message gets passed to each child. As the leader, you may need to share the first "message" to set the pace for the game. Encourage kids to share a whole sentence or two as the message, not just one word. It will help make the point better that way! Make sure each kid gets a turn as the person who starts the message and who ends it.

It is easy for the message to get scrambled in this game! Lots of giggles may ensue over how silly the message becomes! Use this game as a tool to show how much better communication is when it is between just two people. Because of Jesus, we get to speak and listen to God directly! Wow!

Art Project: Prayer Chain

Directions:
Have all the children share a prayer request, questions for God, or parts of the Lord's prayer. Have the children write each child's request on a separate paper strip. Then make a ring with each strip and hook them together (like a paper chain).
Have the children take them home and hang them in their room so they can remember to pray for each request each night.

Supplies:

- Construction paper cut into many strips
- Scissors
- Glue sticks, tape, or staples
- Optional: stickers, glitter

Week 10: Story

We Tell the Story of God

Leader Preparation
Living the Story of God

The idea of "story" means that we understand, experience, and intersect God's story and others' stories. As we learn to see all of life through the gospel lens, we live out our identities by knowing the story we're living, knowing others' stories, listening for "lesser stories," and finding ways to display God's better story in our own lives, in our church family, and in our mission field.

Everybody lives in light of a larger story. They are rehearsing these stories in their minds all of the time, and the stories provide the lenses through which people view their worlds. A person's dominant story will significantly shape his or her beliefs and behaviors and everything in his or her life.

We should all know God's story and rehearse it regularly to ourselves and to one another. We need to be regularly in God's Word, the Bible, to be acquainted with His story. We also need to listen well to others' stories so we can bring the good news of God's redemptive story to bear on the stories of those who don't yet know how God can redeem their brokenness.

See, we understand, experience, and intersect with God's Story and others'. God has been unfolding His Story since before time began. We believe we are participants in the Story and need to understand it and see how our lives intersect with it. Therefore, we regularly reacquaint ourselves with the Story by interacting with God's Word. We look for ways and times to tell the Story often. We also take time to listen to others' stories and help them find their lives within God's Story (Genesis 1:1–2; John 1:1; Psalm 1; 2 Timothy 3:16–17).

How do you see your life as part of God's story? How is He writing your story?

Suggested Lesson Outline

Here's a rough outline for this lesson. It's likely the story, craft, and prayer time will not fill all the time you have with the kids. This extra time is intentional. Free-play time is an important part of kids getting together!

Games, puzzles, or coloring sheets: 10-15 minutes
Get to know the name of each child and build some foundational relationships. It's a good idea to have just a few things out instead of letting the kids get into anything they want in this time. For example, have out just puzzles, or use the coloring sheet for this lesson and have the kids start with coloring.

Review
During this time, engage the kids in what you talked about last week. You can ask the questions in the lesson and/or recite the summary paragraph in the lesson.

Story and discussion: 10 minutes
The story and discussion act like a script and are meant to be relational. They might take only five minutes; it depends on the children. For this story, we highly suggest reading from *The Jesus Storybook Bible* "The Story and the Song" on page 12. You can also watch the video of the same story: https://youtu.be/NN0uX-rdqdU

Theme verse and prayer: 5 minutes
Read the verse. You could ask the kids to stand and stretch, read the verse again, and then pray together.

Activity: 10-15 minutes
The activity is a great time to go over the lesson again or hit points that you were not able to during the "sit down time." It's also a great time to see the lesson take root.

Group game/free play/singing: Remainder of time

> ### Extra Resources
> We've compiled videos, coloring sheets, and additional aids for this lesson and they're easy to use:
> **https://saturatetheworld.com/GB4K-extras**

Review

Teacher's Review: Last week's lesson was about listening to God through prayer. The kids heard Jesus's teaching on prayer and played a game of "Telephone" to practice the rhythm of listening not only to God but also to others.

Ask:	Did anyone remember to pray for the things you wrote down? Did anyone try to pray? How did it go?
Remind:	We get to pray as children of God, servants to Jesus, and missionaries empowered by the Spirit! We get to talk and listen to God!

Diving into the Rhythm of Story

Ask:	What is your favorite story? What do you like about it?
Ask:	Have you ever wondered what the Bible is all about? What kind of book is it?

Story : The Bible is the Story

For this story, we highly suggest reading from *The Jesus Storybook Bible* "The Story and the Song" on page 12.

You can also watch the video of the same story: **https://youtu.be/NN0uX-rdqdU**

Ask:	What is the Bible about? It's the Story of God showing who He is. How does God teach us about Himself?
Ask:	Is the story about heroes?
Ask:	Who is the hero of the story?
Ask:	Is the story about rules?
Explain:	The story is about God and what He has done.
Ask:	What is our story about? What are our lives about?

Read the Theme Verse:

Ephesians 4:1 says, "Therefore . . . lead a life worthy of your calling, for you have been called by God."

Prayer:

Ask the kids if there is anything they want to pray for. Let them pray for one another. As the leader, pray last in light of today's lesson.

Activity: Performing a Play

Have the children create and perform a play. This can be as simple as coming up with the lines and story before acting it out. This activity may seem daunting for them. If it is, choose a story or parable from the life of Jesus, and have them act out that story. Make sure you give every kid a role. As you direct the play, you will likely need to give them their lines and explain each part of the story. We all have a role to play in God's story!

Week II: Bless

We Give and Help Others

Leaders Preparations
Living the Story of God

To "bless" means we intentionally display God's grace through words, gifts, and actions. Followers of Jesus believe we've been blessed with unmerited favor and provision and see our blessings as a means God uses to bless others. We don't truly own anything yet have more than we could have dreamed. We use God's resources for God.

Everybody has been blessed. God's people know they have been blessed to be a blessing. We give from what we have to others in the form of words, actions, or tangible gifts. Such blessing is not meant to be a once-in-a-while deal. God intends for us to live in a perpetual rhythm of blessing others. This truth is one of the distinctive aspects of God's people throughout God's Story. Whatever God gives to His people, He plans to give through them to others who need what they have. We have been blessed to be a blessing.

Another way of saying all of this is: Live in such a way that it would demand a "Jesus explanation." In other words, you wouldn't be able to explain what you do or why without needing to talk about Jesus. That's how followers of Jesus are meant to live. There should be no way to explain our actions without also needing to talk about Jesus.

We intentionally bless others through words, gifts, or actions. God desires that all nations—all people—be blessed through Jesus. Now, as His Body, we believe we live out this mission as we bless others. We intentionally seek God's direction for who He would have us tangibly bless each week (Genesis 12:1–3; Ephesians 1:22–23, 2:8–10; 1 Peter 2:12).

Ask the Spirit to show you who to bless and how to bless them. Listen, and then bless with words, actions, or gifts.

Suggested Lesson Outline

Here's a rough outline for this lesson. It's likely the story, craft, and prayer time will not fill all the time you have with the kids. This extra time is intentional. Free-play time is an important part of kids getting together!

Games, puzzles, or coloring sheets: 10-15 minutes
Get to know the name of each child and build some foundational relationships. It's a good idea to have just a few things out instead of letting the kids get into anything they want in this time. For example, have out just puzzles, or use the coloring sheet for this lesson and have the kids start with coloring.

Review
During this time, engage the kids in what you talked about last week. You can ask the questions in the lesson and/or recite the summary paragraph in the lesson.

Story and discussion: 10 minutes
The story and discussion act like a script and are meant to be relational. They might take only five minutes; it depends on the children.

Theme verse and prayer: 5 minutes
Read the verse. You could ask the kids to stand and stretch, read the verse again, and then pray together.

Art time: 10-15 minutes
The art time is a great opportunity to go over the lesson again or hit points that you were not able to during the "sit down time." Place their art project and coloring sheet into their art box when they finish. At the end of the fourteen weeks, they will take their box home.

Group game/free play/singing: Remainder of time

> ### Extra Resources
> We've compiled videos, coloring sheets, and additional aids for this lesson and they're easy to use:
> https://saturatetheworld.com/GB4K-extras

Review

Teacher's Review: Last week's lesson was about the Bible and how it is a story about God as the hero who makes everything right. It isn't a list of rules or random stories, but one really big drama about God, the world, and people. Ask them what they remember about last week, and remind them we are talking about ways we follow Jesus every day.

Ask them what they remember about last week, and remind them we are talking about ways we follow Jesus every day.

Diving into the Rhythm of Blessing

Ask: Do you remember the story about how Jesus was King and Servant?

Explain: Remember that even though He was God, He got on His hands and knees and cleaned His friends' feet.

Ask: Do you remember what He said at the end? He said to do this for each other. He has made us servants!

Explain: Today we are going to look at what that looks like in everyday life.

Story : The Woman who Blessed Jesus

As you read the story, pause to ask clarifying questions of the kids or offer short explanations as you go.

Six days before the Passover celebration began, Jesus arrived in Bethany, the home of Lazarus—the man He had raised from the dead. A dinner was prepared in Jesus's honor. Martha served, and Lazarus was among those who ate with Him. Then Mary took a twelve-ounce jar of expensive perfume made from essence of nard, and she anointed Jesus's feet with it, wiping His feet with her hair. The house was filled with the fragrance.

But Judas Iscariot, the disciple who would soon betray Him, said, "That perfume was worth a year's wages. It should have been sold and the money given to the poor." Not that he cared for the poor—he was a thief, and since he was in charge of the disciples' money, he often stole some for himself.

Jesus replied, "Leave her alone. She did this in preparation for my burial. You will always have the poor among you, but you will not always have me."

After reading the story, retell it in your own words. This will help the children understand the key themes and moments of the story.

Ask:	Who was the woman in this story?
Ask:	What was she famous for? Being a sinner, not important.
Ask:	How and what did she give to Jesus?
Explain:	She gave her best, most precious thing (perfume). Remind the children of how precious perfume was.
Ask:	How did she serve Jesus?
Explain:	She got on her hands and knees. Remind the kids how selflessly she tried to lavish blessing on Jesus.
	Was all this necessary? Did she have to do this for Jesus? No, but out of her heart, she desired to bless Jesus.
Ask:	Why did she do this? She loved Jesus!
Explain:	Because we are servants, we will do crazy, un-selfish things to bless and help our family, neighbors, friends, and even enemies.
Ask:	What can you do this week to serve someone in a crazy, over-the-top-blessing sort of way?

Help the kids brainstorm how they can help a friend, neighbor, parent, or sibling.

Read the Theme Verse:

Ephesians 4:1 says, "Therefore . . . lead a life worthy of your calling, for you have been called by God."

Prayer:

Ask the kids if there is anything they want to pray for. Let them pray for each other. As the leader, pray last in light of today's lesson.

Art Project: Perfume Bottle

Directions:
Let the kids design and paint their own bottles. Using scissors, the adults punch holes in the top of the bottle and tie a string through it to make a necklace. Explain to the kids that perfume would have been so valuable back then, people would carry it with them like a necklace.

Supplies:
- Small, plastic soda or water bottles (one for each child)Paint
- Markers
- String
- Scissors

Week 12: Celebrate
We Party

Leader Preparation

Celebrate

"Celebration" means that when we gather together, God is the reason we celebrate. Celebrations, festivals, and parties are seen throughout the Bible and history. By seeing God as the reason to celebrate everything, this rhythm asks you to think about what you celebrate and to create times to remember and display the One who is truly worth celebrating.

Everybody engages in some form of celebration, from birthday parties to national holidays. Disciples celebrate the grace of God given to us through Jesus to express how good and gracious God is. As people made in the image of God, we were created to celebrate. God celebrates. He parties! When God created, He celebrated. He said, "This is very good!" God's Word also directs us to celebrate His good work with Him.

God's people look back on what God has done for us through Jesus and forward to what we will enjoy forever in Jesus's presence. We celebrate these blessings. Jesus actually compared His kingdom to a great party (Matthew 22:1–2). One day, we will have an amazing celebration with Jesus at the center of the party (Revelation 19:6–9).

In bringing the better wine to the party at Cana (John 2:1–11), Jesus was bringing what they lacked in a generous and loving way. In stripping down to take on the posture of a servant sent to wash His disciples' feet (John 13:1–11), Jesus was bringing a servant towel for clean up. In the lives of those around us, sometimes there is simply no party where there should be one. As disciples of Jesus, we follow Jesus by bringing what is lacking to the celebrations in our culture.

Let's host parties for friends' birthdays, anniversaries, or accomplishments, and as we do, let's celebrate God's work in and through them (whether they follow Jesus or not!). Let's enjoy holidays, and as we do, let's (for example) give thanks to the Giver of everything in November, celebrate eternal freedom in July, and outright party at Easter. Let's give good gifts; let's "bring the better wine"!

The Kingdom is like a party. We are the party people because we belong to the King who parties. He is the best at celebrating.

What holidays, events, and everyday things do you typically celebrate? Considering the past year, what has each of those celebrations looked like? How could you bring the joy of the gospel into those celebrations this year?

Suggested Lesson Outline

Here's a rough outline for this lesson. It's likely the story, craft, and prayer time will not fill all the time you have with the kids. This extra time is intentional. Free-play time is an important part of kids getting together!

Games, puzzles, or coloring sheets: 10-15 minutes
Get to know the name of each child and build some foundational relationships. It's a good idea to have just a few things out instead of letting the kids get into anything they want in this time. For example, have out just puzzles, or use the coloring sheet for this lesson and have the kids start with coloring.

Review
During this time, engage the kids in what you talked about last week. You can ask the questions in the lesson and/or recite the summary paragraph in the lesson.

Story and discussion: 10 minutes
The story and discussion act like a script and are meant to be relational. They might take only five minutes; it depends on the children.

Theme verse and prayer: 5 minutes
Read the verse. You could ask the kids to stand and stretch, read the verse again, and then pray together.

Art time: 10-15 minutes
The art time is a great opportunity to go over the lesson again or hit points that you were not able to during the "sit down time." Place their art project and coloring sheet into their art box when they finish. At the end of the fourteen weeks, they will take their box home.

Group game/free play/singing: Remainder of time

> ### Extra Resources
> We've compiled videos, coloring sheets, and additional aids for this lesson and they're easy to use:
> https://saturatetheworld.com/GB4K-extras

Review

Teacher's Review: Last week's lesson was about the rhythm of blessing, and the kids learned about the story of the woman who worshiped Jesus and anointed Him with perfume. The lesson ended with children thinking of ways to bless a friend, neighbor, parent, or sibling. Ask them what they remember about last week, and remind them we are talking about ways we follow Jesus every day.

Review Previous Weeks

Ask: Was anyone able to bless a friend, neighbor, parent, or sibling last week?

Ask: What was it like trying to bless someone else?

Explain: Did you remember you were actually serving Jesus?

Diving into the Rhythm of Celebrating

Ask: Have you ever been to a party? What is it like? What do you do at parties?

Explain: Today we're going to talk about how God asks us to celebrate and party.

Story : The Party When the Son Returned[7]

As you read the story, pause to allow for questions and offer short explanations to help the children.

Jesus told them this story: "A man had two sons. The younger son told his father, 'I want my share of your estate now before you die.' So his father agreed to divide his wealth between his sons.

"A few days later this younger son packed all his belongings and moved to a distant land, and there he wasted all his money in wild living. About the time his money ran out, a great famine (when food couldn't grow because there wasn't any rain) swept over the land, and he began to starve. He persuaded a local farmer to hire him, and the man sent him into his fields to feed the pigs.

---

[7] This week's story is directly from Luke 15:11-24, New Living Translation, except for parenthesis which are added to give children clarity.

The young man became so hungry that even the pods he was feeding the pigs looked good to him. But no one gave him anything.

"When he finally came to his senses, he said to himself, 'At home even the hired servants have food enough to spare, and here I am dying of hunger! I will go home to my father and say, "Father, I have sinned against both heaven and you, and I am no longer worthy of being called your son. Please take me on as a hired servant."'

"So he returned home to his father. And while he was still a long way off, his father saw him coming. Filled with love and compassion, he ran to his son, embraced him, and kissed him. His son said to him, 'Father, I have sinned against both heaven and you, and I am no longer worthy of being called your son.'

"But his father said to the servants, 'Quick! Bring the finest robe in the house and put it on him. Get a ring for his finger and sandals for his feet (These are special clothes!). And kill the calf we have been fattening (That means they were going to eat a really good and special meal!). We must celebrate with a feast, for this son of mine was dead and has now returned to life. He was lost, but now he is found.' So the party began."

Retell the story in your own words, and ask the kids to fill in the blanks and help you.

Ask:	Why were they having a party?
Explain:	Because their son had come home! Because the father had welcomed him back and the relationship between the father and son was restored.
Ask:	Why should we party?
Explain:	Jesus came to rescue us. Because God has done good things for us, we have the most to party about! We remember all the good things God has done for His people! He rescued us, saved us, loves us, and sends into the world to be part of restoring it!
Ask:	What has God done for us?
Ask:	What does celebrating God look like?
Explain:	Singing, dancing, talking, sharing, eating, and more —we get together to sing and celebrate. Because God is so good, we have everything to sing about everything to laugh about. God is great and loving. We also throw parties and serve at parties for other people. Being a follower of Jesus means you're a party person.

Read the Theme Verse:

Ephesians 4:1 says, "Therefore . . . lead a life worthy of your calling, for you have been called by God."

Prayer:

Ask the kids if there is anything they want to pray for. Let them pray for each other. As the leader, pray last in light of today's lesson.

Art Project: Banner Streamers

Directions:
Create simple celebratory flags with streamers. Allow the children to select colored streamers, and cut them to their desired length (they can even staple multiple colors onto the same "strip" or glue multiple strips along the pole). Glue the streamer to the pole by applying glue to the pole and wrapping the streamer around. Allow the kids to wave their newly made flags.

Alternative: If you are unsure the kids can play safely with the poles, you can create kites made with strings and streamers instead. You could also use long craft paper to make one large "party" banner, allowing all the kids to decorate it.

Supplies:
- Paper streamers or ribbons in different colors
- Wooden craft dowels/poles (One for each child)
- Glue
- Scissors
- Staples

Week 13: Eat

We Share Meals with Others

Leaders Preparation
Everyday Eating with Gospel Intentionality

"Eating" means we regularly eat meals with others as a display of the love, provision, and acceptance of God. We overcome idols such as selfishness (giving up "family time" and extra cost to feed others), perfection ("the house is a mess"), safety ("they're not like me"), and control (when folks just show up). We "lay down our lives" and invite people in—followers of Jesus or not—and generously share good food and drink with them.

Something very significant happens at a meal. We are hungry. We are in need. That need is met only by something outside of our bodies. It's interesting that Jesus called Himself "the bread of life" (John 6:35). We have a deep spiritual hunger that can be met only by Jesus. When people eat together, they experience something more than a physical event. A spiritual event takes place, whether they acknowledge it or not. God has provided a means to sustain life outside of our own lives, and whenever we eat, we are experiencing God's care and provision.

The meal creates an experience of unity, of oneness at a table. This is why most business deals take place during meals and why more conversation happens when people have drinks in their hands or are sitting together around a table. This is also why Jesus was called a friend of sinners; He identified with them over meals (Matthew 11:19). This is why the Lord's Supper or Eucharist is also called Communion; it is a common meal eaten together to remind us of a common provision we share. We are one in our need and one in taking in God's provision for our need—thus, we have communion.

You're already eating, probably three times a day. Don't do it alone. Do it with others, and watch Jesus join you at the table and change the meal. He's well acquainted with joining people at the table. Invite Him to dinner with a few others and see what He does.

Who can you invite over for a meal?

Suggested Lesson Outline

Here's a rough outline for this lesson. It's likely the story, craft, and prayer time will not fill all the time you have with the kids. This extra time is intentional. Free-play time is an important part of kids getting together!

Games, puzzles, or coloring sheets: 10-15 minutes
Get to know the name of each child and build some foundational relationships. It's a good idea to have just a few things out instead of letting the kids get into anything they want in this time. For example, have out just puzzles, or use the coloring sheet for this lesson and have the kids start with coloring.

Review
During this time, engage the kids in what you talked about last week. You can ask the questions in the lesson and/or recite the summary paragraph in the lesson.

Story and discussion: 10 minutes
The story and discussion act like a script and are meant to be relational. They might take only five minutes; it depends on the children.

Theme verse and prayer: 5 minutes
Read the verse. You could ask the kids to stand and stretch, read the verse again, and then pray together.

Art time: 10-15 minutes
The art time is a great opportunity to go over the lesson again or hit points that you were not able to during the "sit down time." Place their art project and coloring sheet into their art box when they finish. At the end of the fourteen weeks, they will take their box home.

Group game/free play/singing: Remainder of time

> ### Extra Resources
> We've compiled videos, coloring sheets, and additional aids for this lesson and they're easy to use:
> https://saturatetheworld.com/GB4K-extras

Review

Teacher's Review: In the previous lesson, the children learned about the rhythms of celebrating and partying because of God's good gift to us—Jesus. They heard the story of the prodigal son and discussed ways they could party because of the gospel..

Review Previous Weeks

Ask the kids to share what they've learned so far about the gospel. Ask them to share with you what they remember about Jesus, how He lived, and His death and resurrection.

Diving into the Rhythm of Eating

Ask: What is your favorite food? Why?

Explain: Today we're talking about eating. Did you know eating is a big thing Jesus changes when we follow Him?

Story : Meals Remind Us of Jesus

Luke 22:14-20

As you tell this story, you can pause to clarify things and offer short explanations so the kids can stay engaged.

When the time came, Jesus and the apostles sat down together at the table. Jesus said, "I have been very eager to eat this Passover meal with you before my suffering begins. For I tell you now that I won't eat this meal again until its meaning is fulfilled in the Kingdom of God."

Then He took a cup of wine and gave thanks to God for it. Then He said, "Take this and share it among yourselves. For I will not drink wine again until the Kingdom of God has come."

He took some bread and gave thanks to God for it. Then He broke it in pieces and gave it to the disciples, saying, "This is my body, which is given for you. Do this in remembrance of me."

After supper He took another cup of wine and said, "This cup is the new covenant between God and his people—an agreement confirmed with my blood, which is poured out as a sacrifice for you."

Review:	Jesus said, "This bread is like my body."
Ask:	How is it like His body?
Explain:	His body was broken for our sins.
Review:	Jesus also said, "This wine is like my blood, poured out for you."
Ask:	What do you think that meant?
Explain:	Jesus died instead of us!
Ask:	What did Jesus tell us about this meal? Why do we do it?
Explain:	We remember that Jesus rescued us and that we are saved because Jesus loved us so much! That is why we share a meal every time our gospel community gets together. That is why we share communion when we gather on Sundays. God made this meal a reminder to everyone!
Ask:	We don't just eat the meal called communion do we? What other meals do we eat?
	Lead them to acknowledge breakfast, snacks, lunch, and dinner.
Ask:	Why do we have to eat all those meals?
	Lead them to see that if they don't eat, they will be hungry. We need food to live!
Explain:	Food reminds us of our need for God, but it's also through meals that we connect with our families and people outside our families. It's one way we build friendships with others. In fact, in the meal Jesus shared with His disciples, He was actually bringing them into a deep friendship with God—even when they didn't deserve it.
Ask:	How can we eat with others and invite people into friendship with us and God?
	Lead them to think about eating with friends at school or having snack time with others as a way to love people and include them the way Jesus includes us in His meal – the Lord's Supper.

Read the Theme Verse:

Ephesians 4:1 says, "Therefore . . . lead a life worthy of your calling, for you have been called by God."

Prayer:

Ask the kids if there is anything they want to pray for. Let them pray for each other. As the leader, pray last in light of today's lesson.

Art Project: Making Fine Dishes

Directions:
In this activity, the kids will paint and decorate plates and cups for a pretend meal. Tip: Use washable paint and smocks. The kids will love this craft!

Warning: After decorating these plates, they will be beautiful but will not be safe to eat on.

Optional Activity: If you have the space or a play kitchen, have the kids prepare a pretend meal and share it together—like a tea party. You can take turns practicing hospitality.

Supplies:
- Paper plates
- Paper cups
- Paint
- Stickers

Week 14: Recreate
We Play and Enjoy Creation

Leaders Preparation
Everyday Gospel Enjoyment

"Recreate" is our word for the rhythm of "rest and create." Recreating means we take time to rest, play, create, and restore beauty in ways that reflect God to ourselves and to others.

Our God created and then rested. He didn't stop sustaining the universe and take a nap. His rest was a deep satisfaction with what He had created. His creation was very good. If you believe the good news of Jesus Christ, you also are able to truly rest. We can live with the confidence that God is running the world, so we don't have to. We can be settled at heart, knowing Jesus has done all the work necessary to make us acceptable to God, so we no longer need to try to earn His acceptance through our work. We can work with all of our hearts unto the Lord out of gratitude and actually be at rest while we are working.

If we believe the gospel, we can create amazing stuff as an outpouring of our new identity as new-creation people. In fact, those of us who are in Christ should be the most creative people because we have been freed from enslavement to the approval of others, and we are daily becoming more like our Creator. Because He has restored and is restoring us, we are also able to bring restoration to things broken, distorted, or marred by sin. This leads us to work in a state of rest, create at rest, and play at rest.

I have discovered that my lack of faith in God's power to save, sustain, and secure me is displayed in my lack of ability to rest, create, and play. Too many of us can't rest and create. We should be the most playfully rested people on earth because our Dad has it all taken care of for us!

How do you enjoy God's creation through creating and resting?

Suggested Lesson Outline

Here's a rough outline for this lesson. It's likely the story, craft, and prayer time will not fill all the time you have with the kids. This extra time is intentional. Free-play time is an important part of kids getting together!

Games, puzzles, or coloring sheets: 10-15 minutes
Get to know the name of each child and build some foundational relationships. It's a good idea to have just a few things out instead of letting the kids get into anything they want in this time. For example, have out just puzzles, or use the coloring sheet for this lesson and have the kids start with coloring.

Review
During this time, engage the kids in what you talked about last week. You can ask the questions in the lesson and/or recite the summary paragraph in the lesson.

Story and discussion: 10 minutes
The story and discussion act like a script and are meant to be relational. They might take only five minutes; it depends on the children.

Theme verse and prayer: 5 minutes
Read the verse. You could ask the kids to stand and stretch, read the verse again, and then pray together.

Art time: Art Show - 10-15 minutes
Give the children space to set up their art projects from the entire 14 weeks so their parents can come and see them. Then, at the end of the lesson, invite the adults in the community to come and see all they made.

Group game/free play/singing: Remainder of time

> ### Extra Resources
> We've compiled videos, coloring sheets, and additional aids for this lesson and they're easy to use:
> https://saturatetheworld.com/GB4K-extras

Review

In the previous lesson, the children learned about sharing meals and the rhythm of eating in the Story of God and in their own lives. They heard the story of the Last Supper and discussed the meaning of this meal and why Jesus gave us food to remind us of the gospel.

Review Previous Weeks

Ask: What is our gospel life?

Explain: Our life with God is filled with eating, parties, gift-giving, helping, story-telling, and praying! What we mean by gospel life is that everything in our lives changes when we receive the good news about Jesus. We still eat, but we eat differently; we still give gifts, but we give gifts differently. Today is the last main lesson in gospel life.

Diving into the Rhythm of Recreating

Our last lesson is to talk about playing. Because of Jesus, we play differently.

Ask: What do you like to do when you play?

Ask: What is your favorite game?

Ask: How do you play with others?

Explain: In the Bible, "play" might best be described as creating and resting, enjoying the world God made, and being the people God made us to be. To play is to follow God in making things and to relax knowing God is in control.

STORY : God Plays in Creation

Read with enthusiasm and excitement. You can also stop to ask clarifying questions or offer short explanations.

In the beginning, God created the heavens and the earth. God, the main character of this story, is the personal, all-powerful being who made everything that exists. He is the true ruler of the universe—lovingly providing for all that is under His care.

The kingdom, or sphere of authority, that God set up was not restricted to the heavens, but God powerfully, intentionally, and creatively spoke all of creation into existence.

He precisely laid the foundations of the earth.

He intentionally separated the waters from the land, filling that land with beautiful flowers and unique animals.

He splashed His creative canvas with many colors and fragrances that all declared His worth.

In five days, God masterfully set up a physical kingdom that was separate from Him, yet uniquely and personally cared for by Him. At the end of each day, God reflected on His work, saying, "It is good."

On the sixth day, God created the first people. God said, "Let us make man in our image," and He formed the dust of the ground together and breathed into it the breath of life. The first humans were created and placed in a perfect garden where they could enjoy the good reign of this God. The people were decidedly different than the rest of creation in that they were given the responsibility of caring for the creation. God spoke to this first man, Adam, and told him to enjoy all He had created: the animals, the flavors, the sights, and the work. Adam and all the humans were created with the ability to enjoy this wonderful environment God had fashioned. They were also created with the great task of reflecting the King's goodness and greatness throughout all of creation.

God made it clear to Adam there were two trees in the center of the garden. One was the Tree of Life. The fruit from this tree was to be enjoyed and eaten just like the rest of the trees. The other tree, known as the Knowledge of Good and Evil, was the only tree from which they were not to eat. If Adam ate of this tree, he would surely die.

This conversation between Adam and God continued as God described what it should look like for Adam to live in this garden. Adam had responsibilities to cultivate the garden and name the animals, operating under God's authority to cultivate the world.

Adam went about the work God gave him to do. As he worked, God said it was not good for man to be alone—he needed a helper. God caused a deep sleep to come over Adam, and by taking a rib from his side He created a woman named Eve for Adam to enjoy, love, protect, care for, and work alongside in relationship. When Adam woke up, he broke into poetry and declared how amazed he was by what God had created. This first marriage was enjoyed without shame and guilt; they were naked in every sense and not the least bit afraid of rejection. God commissioned both the man and the woman with the tasks of cultivating the potential in His creation and multiplying their family by having kids. After the sixth day and the creation of man in His own image, God reflected, "It is very good!"

Then on the seventh day, God rested and reflected on the goodness of His creation. This was not the end of God's relationship with His creation, but rather it was only the beginning. Each day God would come down in the cool of the day and talk with Adam and Eve, teaching them the best possible way to live life and showing them how to live under His good reign. Adam and Eve were able to enjoy both the goodness and greatness of their Creator and His creation.

They worked faithfully in the garden, cultivating it and developing its potential to bring glory to God. They lived in perfect harmony in their relationships with God, His world, and each other.

Ask:	Did it sound like God had fun creating the world? Why did He create the world?
Explain:	He loved making the world and wanted to make something good. He made it for us to live in and enjoy! WOW!
Ask:	Why did He make people? He wanted to share His joy.
Ask:	What did the story call people? God's children
Ask:	What does that make you think of? We are family!
Ask:	If God made the world for us to enjoy, are we enjoying it? What would it look like for us to make beautiful things like God did?
Explain:	God calls us to enjoy creation like Adam and Eve, to walk with Him in every part of life, and to enjoy God's work. That's what the gospel life is all about!

Read the Theme Verse:

Ephesians 4:1 says, "Therefore . . . lead a life worthy of your calling, for you have been called by God."

Prayer:

Ask the kids if there is anything they want to pray for. Let them pray for each other. As the leader, pray last in light of today's lesson.

Activity: Celebrate Your Creative Work

Rest! They've made a lot of artwork, so now it's time to show it off to others. Coordinate with the adults, and have the kids show their parents all the beautiful things they have made in the box, like an art show! After the art show, have the children take their art box home.

Appendix 1:

Speaking the Gospel with Children
by Mirela Watson

We are on the second round of *Frozen* frenzy at our house. Our middle child, Maitê, has one outfit these days: an Elsa dress costume. She knows the words to most of the music and the dialogues and makes similar gestures as princess Elsa. I think most of my patience with this stage comes from two things: 1) Jesus gives me a daily dosage of grace, and 2) I know that this, too, shall pass.

Recently, her little brother was trying to climb on the couch to pester his sister when Maitê pushed him down. He bonked his head on the floor. She immediately got reprimanded for it, and while being disciplined, she started to sing, "Don't let them in. Don't let them see. Be the good girl you always have to be." I was not about to miss a great opportunity to debunk one of Disney's greatest myths and share the gospel of Jesus with her. I looked at her, and the following conversation took place:

"Maitê, did you know this song is not true? Nobody is good."

"Mom, Elsa is good!"

"No, sweetie. She isn't. Nobody is good, not even Elsa. Does she always treat her sister kindly?"

"No, she doesn't."

"Elsa does not always do good things. Her heart is not always good, and her actions are not always good. Are you a good girl?"

"Yes, I am."

"No, sweetie. You're not."

"Yes, Mom, I am!"

"Maitê, did you just get mad at your brother and push him down the couch?"

"Yes, I did."

"Is that a good thing to feel and do?"

"No, Mom."

"The only person who actually has a good heart and does good things is Jesus. Nobody else in the world is good."

She just stared at me, moved on, and kept singing her song.

Often, we think children can't understand the messages around them, and that includes theology and the message of the gospel. Sometimes we try to bring it "down to their level" with arts and crafts and Bible songs, when in reality, all they need is a message that says, "You need a Savior, and Jesus is the only one."

The world is already teaching our children all sorts of gospels: the gospel of "you deserve," the gospel of "you need," and the gospel of "if you behave well and do good things, you are a good person, and life will go well for you." Children understand concepts of right and wrong and good and bad at an early age.

Their cry tells us they are not happy about something. Their laughter gives us joy, and for a follower of Jesus, the reality that our children understand the gospel of Jesus Christ fills our hearts and brings tears of joy to our eyes. In the journey of discipling our children, I have found a few things that help them understand who this Jesus is in whom Mom and Dad believe. It is our hope and prayer that through these conversations, they will love and discover Jesus for themselves.

1) Keep it simple and short.

I am really good at "preaching" to my kids, especially to my six-year-old. When I get on "three-points" mode, I am pretty sure all she hears is her voice saying, "What do I need to say to make Mom stop talking now?" I have found it is in the short, direct, and simple day-to-day conversations that she has a clearer glimpse of Jesus. If you find yourself "preaching" at your child for more than one minute, you've lost their attention.

2) Enter their world, and use words they understand.

My oldest admires Rosa Parks, so a lot of our conversations about the gospel involve Rosa Parks, the desire she had to bring justice, and how she stood up for what was right, even when everyone around her was complying to the law of the time. We often talk about how God is a God who loves justice and wants to see broken things made right. Sometimes I think she understands, and I always wonder how amazed she will be when she fully comprehends the depth of the justice and righteousness Jesus brings to our lives, both here and in eternity.

3) Use the Bible.

The Bible is key. It is the word of God that has the power to transform our lives, and we must use it. The New Living Translation is an "easy read" for older children, and *The Jesus Storybook Bible* is a great resource for younger minds. We have used multiple stories from *The Jesus Storybook Bible* in daily conversations with our children, and it has helped bridge the understanding of their current reality and the impact of the gospel in it.

4) Remember that Jesus is present in every moment of your life and of your children's lives.

I have found that telling my children that Jesus is with them in their daily lives at school, while they are sleeping, while they are playing with their friends, or simply while they are watching a show is comforting in times of fear and distress, and convicting in times of repentance. The Spirit does the work in our lives and in our children's lives, and more often than we think, their hearts are extremely tender to His voice. Encourage your children to speak to Jesus (without you being the mediator) because He listens.

When I was having the conversation earlier with my daughter, my husband overheard it and later on commented on my directness with Maitê. I have found that speaking to our children about Jesus and speaking to Jesus as if He is in fleshly person in our house helps them and us live our lives with an awareness of His presence, His doing, and His love for us.

The gospel of Christ is for the little ones. May we always remember that the simple and pure work of God starts in the simple and pure of heart. In the words of Jesus, "O Father, Lord of heaven and earth, thank you for hiding these things from those who think themselves wise and clever, and for revealing them to the childlike. Yes, Father, it pleased you to do it this way!" (Matthew 11:25b–26).

APPENDIX II

Teaching Our Children to Pray
by Jeff Vanderstelt

As I lead our family devotional time at the dinner table, I have started to use the four questions: Who is God? What has He done? Who are we? What do we do? Not only are these questions great guides through the Biblical text, but our answers can also be helpful guides toward prayer.

Who is God?

What do we know about who God is from this text? I encourage my children to stop and pray prayers of adoration and praise:

God, we praise you because you are so powerful. God, you are the Creator of all things. God, you are in control.

What has He Done?

What does this text show that God has done or is doing? How is He doing that in our lives today? We then take time to pray prayers of thanksgiving for how God was and is at work:

God, you have provided great gifts for us, especially Jesus. God, you gave us a sunny day today. Thank you for the sunshine. Thank you for being in control of our lives and circumstances. You have done many good things for us, such as providing our home, our friends, and our healthy bodies to play sports.

Who are We?

What does this text say is true of us? Are we living like we believe it? Where we are not living in line with the truth of our new identity in Christ, we take some time to confess who God says we are and how we've fallen short. We pray prayers, such as:

God, you say we are your children whom you love very much, but we don't always act like loving children to others. Forgive us and help us to love others like you loved us in Jesus. God, you say we are your creation and that you did good work in making us, but we don't always believe that about ourselves or others. Forgive us and help us to see ourselves and others like you do.

What Do We Do?

If we believed these truths about God, God's work, and our new identity in Christ, what would we do? I encourage my kids to be very specific. As they share, I guide each of them to turn their answer into a prayer of supplication, asking God to help them to obey Him:

God, I want to love my sisters better. Help me to think of them and their needs and not just what I want. God, I really get anxious and worried about my grades. Help me to trust that you are in control even of my grades and not to give in to fear. God, help me to be a better friend to my classmates who are often left alone without a friend.

By directing their answers toward prayer, I am able to lead them in prayers of adoration, thanksgiving, confession, and supplication, and each of their prayers is grounded in the character and work of God in Christ and, as a result, their new identity.

Appendix III
Using the Bible Project Videos for Stories

Some of the stories can be substituted with or enhanced by videos from The Bible Project (https://thebibleproject.com) or with videos from Saturate. Here is an outline of videos that work well with these lessons.

Week 1: The Image of God by The Bible Project

Week 2: The Gospel According to Mark by The Bible Project

Week 3: The Atonement by The Bible Project

Week 4: The Gospel of the Kingdom by The Bible Project

Week 5: Baptismal Identity by Saturate

Week 7: Messiah by The Bible Project

Week 8: Holy Spirit by The Bible Project

Week 9: Shema by The Bible Project

Appendix IV
Using *The Jesus Storybook Bible* for Stories

Some of the stories can be substituted or enhanced with stories from *The Jesus Storybook Bible*. Here's an outline of stories that work well with these lessons.

Week 1: Read "The Beginning: A Perfect Home" from *The Jesus Storybook Bible* on page 18.

Week 2: Read "The Terrible Lie" from *The Jesus Storybook Bible* on page 28.

Week 3: Read "The Sun Stops Shining" from *The Jesus Storybook Bible* on page 302.

Week 4: Read "Going Home" from *The Jesus Storybook Bible* on page 318.

Week 5: Read "Let's Go!" from *The Jesus Storybook Bible* on page on 208. Then read "The Man Who Didn't Have Any Friends" on page 264.

Week 6: Read "Son of Laughter" from *The Jesus Storybook Bible* on page 56.

Week 7: Read "The Servant King" from *The Jesus Storybook Bible* on page 286.

Week 8: Read "Going Home" from *The Jesus Storybook Bible* on page 318.

Week 9: Read "How to Pray" from *The Jesus Storybook Bible* on page 222.

Week 10: Read "The Story and the Song" from *The Jesus Storybook Bible* on page 12.

Week 11: Read "Washed with Tears" from *The Jesus Storybook Bible* on page 280.

Week 12: Read "Get Ready!" from *The Jesus Storybook Bible* on page 170.

Week 13: Read the communion section from *The Jesus Storybook Bible* on page 292.

Week 14: Read "The Beginning: A Perfect Home" from *The Jesus Storybook Bible* on page 18.

The Story of God for Kids

From Creation to Restoration.
The unfolding story of God's creation, redemption, and restoration captivates every human heart-especially the hearts of kids! Telling the Story of the Bible disciples our children better than any other approach. These twenty-two stories guide kids through the key turning points of Scripture and help them learn to engage, discuss, and connect the dots of the Story.

The Story of God for Kids is a proven resource that has helped many children understand the full narrative of the Bible. It's designed for K-5th graders, but can also be used in communities who want to mix adults and kids together and is an excellent way for families to engage the story of God together.

BONUS! Free downloadable coloring pages.
GET A FREE PRINT COPY MAILED TO YOU OR DOWNLOAD A PDF VERSION FOR IMMEDIATE ACCESS.

https://saturatetheworld.com/resource/story-god-kids-curriculum

More Books From

Print Books:

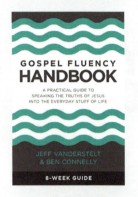
Gospel Fluency Handbook

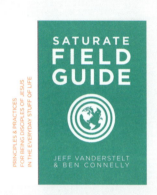
Saturate Field Guide

GICT: Leader Guide   GICT: Participant Guide

eBooks:

But, How Do We Do It?

Our Common Struggle

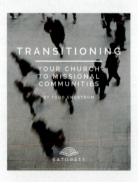
Transitioning Your Church to Missional Communities

available at

www.saturatetheworld.com/books